FIGHTING COCKS

Forty Years of Pennine Poets

Mind and Body

SELECTED AND INTRODUCED BY

K.E. Smith

Edited by Pauline Kirk

Fighting Cock Press

Published by Fighting Cock Press 2006

Fighting Cock Press
45, Middlethorpe Drive,
York YO24 1NA

Editor: Pauline Kirk

Printed by Peepal Tree Press
Original Fighting Cock Logo by Stanley Chapman
Original typing by K.E. Smith
Typeset by Pauline Kirk

Introductory matter © K.E. Smith

ISBN: 0-906744-29-6

www.penninepoets.co.uk

Fighting Cock Press and the Pennine Poets gratefully
acknowledge financial support from the Arts Council
England, and ENDpapers of York.

FIGHTING COCKS

Forty Years of Pennine Poets

In memory of my sister Shirley –
for her love, her kindness and her commonsense

CONTENTS

Birches, from *On Wilsden Hill*, K.E. Smith, 1984, Ian M. Emberson.

Acknowledgements

Every reasonable effort has been made to trace all the poets and artists who have been connected with the Pennine Poets but inevitably, over four decades, there have been sad losses through death, or people have moved and contact has been lost. Several have, therefore, had to be omitted from this anthology, as we have been unable to obtain permission to reprint their work. Should there be readers who were themselves once Pennine Poets, or know that a member of their family was, we would be delighted if they would contact Fighting Cock Press. We will then be able to include their work in any subsequent edition. Thanks are due to the editors of the following journals, anthologies and individual collections, in which some of the poems in this book have previously appeared.

Aireings, Pennine Platform, Platform, Volt.
Pennine Anthology, ed. Joan Lee, 1969.
Pennine Anthology 1980, ed. Alec Smith, 1980.
Pennine Poets Anthology 1966-1986, Fighting Cock Press, 1991.
Pennine 25 Anthology 1966-1991, Fighting Cock Press, 1991.
Pennine Poets Chapbook No. 1: A Taste of the Pennine Poets, Fighting Cock Press, 1995.
Pennine Tracks, ed. Clare Chapman, Fighting Cock Press, 1996.
Poets are People: The Pennine Poets, BBC Radio Leeds and the John Taylor Teachers' Centre, 1976.
The Pennine Poets: Our Poems, Your Poems, BBC Radio Leeds and the John Taylor Teachers' Centre, 1978.
Webbed Skylights of Tall Oaks, Fighting Cock Press, 2002.
An Island Chapter, Anna Adams, Littlewood Press, 1983.
Dear Vincent, Anna Adams, Littlewood Press, 1986.
An Invitation to Supper, Nicholas Bielby, Outposts Publications, 1978.
Remember Wyatt, Nicholas Bielby, Fighting Cock Press, 1999.
Between Clouds and Caves, Pat Borthwick, Littlewood Press, 1988.
The Hot Blizzard, Clare Chapman, Smith/Doorstop Books, 1986.

Dunegrass, Clare Chapman, Fighting Cock Press, 1997.

Headhunters, Cal Clothier, The Ryder Press, 1974.

Bloodmark, Cal Clothier, [n.p.], 1979.

Death Mask, Cal Clothier, Rivelin Press, 1981.

Picasso's Child, Julia Deakin, 2001.

Sunday Afternoon and Other Poems, Gordon H. Dyson, Outposts Publications, 1979.

Swallows Return, Ian M. Emberson, Envoi Poets, 1986.

Three Brontë Poems, Ian M. Emberson, Angria Press, 1993.

Pirouette of Earth, Ian M. Emberson, University of Salzburg, 1995.

Natural Light, Ian M. Emberson, Fighting Cock Press, 1998.

The Rainbow, Gerald England, Fighting Cock Press, 1980.

Futures, Gerald and Christine England, Magic Pen Press, 1986.

Limbo Time, Gerald England, New Hope International, 1998.

Scathed Earth, Mabel Ferrett, University of Salzburg, 1996.

Opus 1, Howard Frost, 1994.

Wakeful in the Sleep of Time, Brian Merrikin Hill, Taxus Press, 1984.

Local History, Brian Merrikin Hill, Littlewood Press, 1985.

Dolphins and Outlaws, Brian Merrikin Hill, University of Salzburg, 1993.

Quite Translated , Neville Hodgson, Arc and Throstle Press, 1978.

Best of Neighbours, Glyn Hughes, Ceolfrith Press, 1979.

The Absent Lord, Trevor Innes, Fighting Cock Press, 1989.

Owlstone, Pauline Kirk, Thalia Press, 2002.

Walking to Snailbeach, Pauline Kirk, Redbeck Press, 2004.

The Mermaid's Purse, Joan Lee, [n.d.p.].

Brakken City, Linda Marshall, Fighting Cock Press, 1997.

A Perfect Spit at the Stars, Lesley Quayle, Spanna in the Works, 1999.

Kingfisher Days, Mary Sheepshanks, Fighting Cock Press, 1998.

Thinning Grapes, Mary Sheepshanks, Fighting Cock Press, 2001.

Horcum and Other Gods, Colin Simms, Headland Publications, 1974.

On Wilsden Hill, K.E. Smith, Fighting Cock Press, 1984.

Ancestral Memories, K.E. Smith, Feather Books, 2002.

Snow Children, S.L.Henderson Smith, Mitre Press, 1968.
Transparencies, S.L. Henderson Smith, Outposts Publications, 1980.
Thornton in Craven and Other Places, Albert Thornton, Society of Civil Service Authors, 1996.
Cat's Cradle, Joyce Thornton, Poetry Workshop, 1986.
Garlic Lane, John Waddington-Feather, Feather Books, 1998.
Breathing Space, Josie Walsh, Ox-Eye Press, 2004.

Our thanks are also due to all who have contributed in any way to the publication of this book, particularly to those whose detective work located several 'missing' Pennine Poets – whose valuable work would otherwise have been omitted from the anthology. Photographs in the introduction are reproduced by kind permission of Nicholas Bielby, Pauline Kirk and the *Spenborough Guardian*.

KES
2006

ILLUSTRATIONS

**The Pennine Poets at the West Yorkshire Playhouse: l. to r.,
Brian Merrikin Hill, Albert Thornton, Nicholas Bielby, Pauline Kirk,
Mabel Ferrett, Clare Chapman, Pat Borthwick.**

INTRODUCTION

Poetry in Our Time

No. Yes. These are both possible answers to the question 'do most people read contemporary poetry?' Clearly no, because even an established poet or a national magazine like *Poetry Review* may at best sell a few thousand copies. (Once-in-a-decade exceptions like Ted Hughes's *Birthday Letters* confirm this general rule). It would not be difficult for most of us to think of lively-minded, cultured friends who could only mention Heaney and, if pushed, Duffy and Armitage, amongst living poets. But also and equally strongly the answer is 'yes' – people do read, and find that they need, modern poetry. Go through some extreme life-event of falling in love or losing someone we love, as all of us must, and the perspective on poetry is liable to change. Suddenly, odd lines from poems we see in the paper or in anthologies may become important for us. Or, just as surprisingly, a friend encloses a poem which has meant a great deal to her or him, hoping it will also help us. And in the aftermath of such life-changing events, many of us begin to set up our own secret hoard of poems written by our contemporaries that speak to our condition.

My hope in editing this book is that I can help lower this 'threshold' of approaching modern poetry a little, so that readers can encounter and enjoy the poems in the run of their normal lives rather than just in the more extreme moments. Or, if you will, that I can attract more people to poetry before they discover a desperate need for it. I believe that many readers may have been put off by reasons which aren't really the fault of the poetry itself. Perhaps they had been made to feel that poetry was something separate from real life, something that needed a special 'poetry voice' to speak it. Or perhaps they had been told that modern poetry was specially difficult, an art-form that required a PhD and a skeleton key to unlock its meanings. Or perhaps they had simply felt that in some way poetry, unlike say jazz or film, was seriously uncool, irrelevant to the rhythms of the culture they inhabited.

I am confident that the poets included here can overcome any such predispositions through their humanity, accessibility and memorable language. But I also trust the layout of this anthology will further help to make the poetry approachable. Its thematic approach means that readers can perhaps take one section of poems that relates to the issues they are concerned with at the time – with changing family life, with our precarious environment, with the North-South divide, with spirituality in a scientific age – and explore it from a variety of viewpoints. They will find that the poems offer something beyond that division between technocratic know-how and a 'vox pop' response to the world, which is what our culture seems to offer us.

The division into themed sections should also help overcome the barrier that a new poetry book can present to readers used to novels or biographies laid out in a clear order of chapters. Presented with a long list of poems by one or several authors, a new reader of modern poetry may wonder how to set about it – should I read this book of poems right through, or one at a time or what? Here the opportunity is offered to read a section of poems in the way one might read a short-story or novel chapter at one sitting before inserting a bookmark for the next time. I would like to think that each section has its own shape, its own beginning, middle and end. Yet my contribution can only be to showcase the poets included here and it is their work which counts. If I can help to lower the general 'threshold' of readers' approach to contemporary poetry, that will be a start. But if I can also introduce the reader to a particularly talented group of poets working in Yorkshire over the last four decades and dramatizing for us the form and pressure of our age, then I shall feel I have achieved something worthwhile.

My First Acquaintance...

The year in which I joined the Pennine Poets, was a strange but memorable one. The history books tell of hyperinflation, of crisis in the economy, of Britain needing an international loan and of simmering social conflict that would lead to a whole winter of discontent within a few short years. But 1976 was also the most glorious summer of the century, not just through day after day but through month after month which ripened the wheat, propped house-doors open and let children play into the long, northern evenings. And in the political world too, despite those ominous clouds of conflict on the horizon, it was a time of hope. As I steadied myself to knock on a solid Victorian door in Heckmondwike where I knew only that the workshop group called the Pennine Poets met every month, I felt an underlying optimism. Despite my anxiety about the quality of my own writing, my worry about what this new set of people would think of it, I was buoyed up by hope.

Society, I felt, would soon move decisively away from selfish materialism to foster the creativity of the individual. Poetry could play an important role in bringing that better world into being. And the poetry group I was about to join would be a place to share this heady optimism. If all this seems hopelessly naïve some thirty years later, I can only say that hindsight is a wonderfully clever thing. But I remain eternally grateful that, right from that fine summer of 1976 to the present, the Pennine Poets at least have exceeded my naïve, youthful expectations. They remain much of the reason I still retain some of those hopes for a better world to this day.

Let me try and share with you the general atmosphere of the Pennine Poets then and since. My aim is not to offer a detailed history of a group which was already a decade old when I joined it (Mabel Ferrett has ably done that in a companion volume, *Spirit and Emotion*), but to convey something of its 'feel'. As with any close human grouping some things about it have changed radically, while other things have endured. So what things *have* remained consistent? First, of course, like all successful writing groups, the Pennine Poets have had a commitment to the art of writing itself. People of different beliefs and with different ways of writing poetry have been able to come together for detailed, rigorous yet sympathetic comments on the poems they have read out. Always the emphasis has been on accepting the poet's own starting point and then trying to help her or him articulate what was really intended but not quite expressed first time round.

The second consistent factor has been the sheer range of people who have come. Professional in their attitude to poetry, they have often had demanding 'day jobs' as well which have informed their writing – from their perspectives as teachers, social workers, housepersons, journalists, artists, carers and a host of other occupations. This variety of inputs has been increased by a wide geographical catchment area, with writers travelling from York, Leeds, Todmorden and Manchester to Heckmondwike, on rainy as well as sunny Friday evenings.

But then again, what has changed about the group? Well, as I have suggested, in those earlier years there was a lot of hopeful debate about the arts and society. Like other thoughtful people we were responding as citizens to that conflictual period in British life, but we were also trying as writers to get beyond the headlines to the deeper causes involved, to use our creative imaginations to access a deeper, shared humanity. Out of that came some very fine poetry which was not party-political but was deeply engaged in the quest for social justice. As Brian Merrikin Hill wrote in 'The Bridge':

We have not lost paradise; it was never found.
We are always seeking.

It is true that the quest for a shared humanity that started in the Sixties and Seventies has gone on ever since in writing as elsewhere – one has only to think of the continuing struggle for equal expression among women, people with disabilities or ethnic minorities. But, as we all know, in the 1980s many things changed in British society and these changes were bound to affect the Pennine Poets too. It is probably fair to say that the relative collapse of some of the older radical causes in the early 1980s, and a sense that material values were all, caused a crisis of confidence in the role of the arts in Britain. But this was compensated for from the later 1980s on by a new involvement of poetry in the contemporary world of work, consumption, the media and popular culture. Younger Pennine Poets would be as at home in this shifting, new world as the New Generation 'stars' Carol Ann Duffy or Simon Armitage, and as able to make creative poetry from their encounter with it. Linda Marshall's isolated lovers in 'Incompatible' are very much of our consumer culture:

> He could not stop buying rainbows.
> She would pay anything for the stars.
> There were rainbows on his combs,
> His shirts, his sheets, his wristwatch.
> She had a moon on her shoes, a star
> On her scarf, constellations dangling
> From her ears.

A key point about the Pennine Poets, which has remained consistent throughout these changes, is that they have always remained engaged with the issues of their time. Yet poetry must offer us something slower-burning and more sustaining than journalism in terms of helping us to live in a changing present. Poetry, as Ezra Pound said, is news that stays news. It offers us a chance to connect the particulars of our life with more universal truths, not to escape our history but to be able to stand back from it, and create a larger story that can give a firm narrative to events and to our role within them. It is the very fact of our living in a news-bombarded, 24/7 global village that has made the imaginative and reflective aspects of poetry even more important. In this anthology we shall see how the work of the Pennine Poets has helped continue this vocation of poets as the antennae of the human race. And what better starting point for our journey of discovery than the Pennine Poets' own 'home county'?

Yorkshires of the Mind

A sense of place. It is such a hard thing to define yet it is surely always important to us. Just to think of its opposite – the feeling of something soulless and alien – is to grasp why it matters so much. To have a sense of place is to feel the past in the present, to see the natural and the human mingled, to connect all these with one another. Relating to this connected web of location, people, scenery and history also helps strengthen our own personal identities. Poetry is the ideal medium for conveying such a sense of place just because it condenses disparate impressions into memorable wholes. When we arrive in a new place we often have a total impression that is more than the sum of its parts. This sense of rich strangeness is captured by Clare Chapman in 'Driving Home on a Moor' as she describes the untamed power of the moors at night – even through the glass of our protective capsules:

> It is the car's movement that creates the wind,
> Compounds of lead and carbon buckle grass
> But over us a war, conflict of cloud,
> A monarch swirling a cape,
> A tumbling of wool,
> Our voices wither under this boiling.

But still the idea of 'Yorkshire' as a whole might be more of a problem to grasp than the idea of, say, Wetwang or Whitby. Its sheer size and diversity, from the Humber to the Pennines, make it less easy to envisage than other English counties. As myself a 'Yorkshireman born and bred' I am aware that my own image of the county is very personal and partial. Brought up in the industrial-rural South Pennines I yet discover in myself a special affection for the county's far north-western, limestone fringes where Ingleborough guards the passage between Yorkshire and the Lakes. But the county is a region in itself and everyone, whether 'native' or incomer has a right to their own personal Yorkshire.

Naturally, one response of the Pennine Poets to this diversity has been to celebrate and dramatize it. We can enter into the turbulent riverscape in Mabel Ferrett's 'Humber Bridge' to be reminded both of human ambition and of its transience:

> Under the arch the waters boil
> in runnels, deep where force meets force,
> confronting of the ocean surge
> with river's downward thrusting course,
> eternal warring, surf and soil;
> the bridge that for a span rides both...

Or we can share in a quieter but equally profound exploration of time-zones – as between an ancient limestone landscape and the current lives of martins and hawthorns in Ian Emberson's 'Malham Cove':

> Cream curve
> of the sealess sea cliffs
> of the sealess cove,
> where houseless martins
> gull-glide the green green waves,
> and hawthorn flowers
> and fingering leaves of ash
> crash-cry upon its limestone precipice.

Yet these diverse impressions do, I think, have something in common which we can locate as particularly 'Yorkshire' and which is unusual in the small, crowded country of England. It is a sense of extent, of rich spread and sprawl, of space spreading out from small details to large vistas of time. In his free sonnet 'Lister's Mill' John Cook deliberately takes 'This distant view' of the mill's 'square Victorian lines and scale'. He then moves further out, to where nineteenth-century Yorkshire gives way to twenty-first century Yorkshire, to 'lean new turbines gleaning the moorland winds'. All these poems put down tap-roots into history, whether recently-human or distantly-geological. As Cal Clothier reminds us in 'Huddersfield' there is always a rich traffic between the solid stones around us and the inner stories we tell of them:

> There is the town of stone,
> of wool and history, that solid place where I once lived;
> and then there is the town which lives in me
> and like the town which lived my childhood out,
> it lines my veins and rings my trunk, and has a root
> deep in the way I move towards tomorrow.

John Waddington-Feather's poetic interludes in his play *Garlic Lane* capture powerfully for us the town in which he lived his childhood (Keighley) but also creates a memorable archetype of all Yorkshire and Lancashire mill-towns in their industrial heyday. It is important in the end to remind ourselves that all our boundaries and frontiers, including those of Yorkshire itself, are both real and arbitrary, following actual contour lines yet also being creations of our own minds. They really exist out there, beyond our own transitory beings, yet their life and their meaning survive only in our shared memory and imagination. Beyond Barnoldswick was once the county border with Lancashire. Now Barnoldswick itself has dropped into Lancashire – or has it rather in spirit remained, as in Albert Thornton's 'Barnoldswick via Colne', poised on Yorkshire's edge?:

> All must have been Flat Earth Folk
> the train stopped here, a single line,
> outward was push and coming home was pull – so
> miss the train – walk off the edge and fall
> into The Unknown Land that's Lancashire.

All this rich sense of history should not take us away from the fact that the poet's own experience is of a particular here-and-now. The Yorkshire of these writers is a rich composite of such present moments. The year wheels from the sharp illumination of Pauline Kirk's 'Beyond Leathley':

> Celandines splash light; a milky way of wood aven
> glows beside a stream. Yet even in this quiet haven
> winter debris strews the scene

round to 'That Day' when Gerald England finds delight in 'low November sun':

> Gillamoor looked great that day,
> the done-heather brown over the hillside,
> bare trees exposing the moor to view.

To have a sense of place is both to grasp one's own transience and to gain a sense of something greater. In the end Yorkshire is the familiar place where the poet lives but it is also the key to understanding that one's address ends with the universe – as we knew when we wrote our name and address in our first school-books:

> And we are passing moments, cradled
> Between steep banks, our grandeur lives:
>
> Impassioned, frail – yet intimating
> How all things are held together.

These 'Thoughts on the River Nidd' by Linda Marshall bring us back to the integrating role that a loved place can bring, not by denying the frailty of our individual lives but by giving to those lives both depth and wholeness. But if, as T. S. Eliot once wrote 'home is where we start from', the next question is: where are we and our poets starting out *for*? Life, we often say rather glibly, is a journey in itself and within that metaphorical journey we make many literal journeys. Ours is an age of travel, to be sure, but what do we hope to find when we arrive at our destination? And how, if at all, do those expectations square with the reality?

Ian M. Emberson.

Pilgrimages

If poetry can bring out the strangeness and wonder of 'home' it can also bring the world of cheap air-travel and alluring destinations back to more basic human realities. For the best 'travel-poems' are much more than travel-poems. They are, in Brian Merrikin Hill's phrase, 'poems of pilgrimage'. Simultaneously, a poem like Hill's 'The Bridge' explores both psychological and geographical journeys, landscapes of the mind and of nature. The poet shares with us the recognizable world of 'holiday' but his journey is not the one mapped out by the tour company, the driver or the guidebook:

> Between bends the road crosses the turbulent falls
> hustling blue Morar to the lucid strait.
> The driver glimpses red weed, white beach, recalls
> the guidebook: 'More silver sand. Did you see the
> > boat?
> The lake is up that road to the right, dead end
> far off the route. Can you hear the torrent roar?'
> They pass on, they ignore
> the source, life's ground –
> the calm baptismal water lapping the strand,
> the mysterious holy hills of the further shore.

Often, as here, the Pennine Poets seek to explore what was once known as 'the matter of Britain'. Today we might term it the mental mapping of 'home', of an island archipelago off continental Europe which is at once familiar and strange. On the one hand, this relatively small country is extremely well-known and well-mapped. On the other, because it has in the past functioned as the 'centre' of a large empire, its apparently familiar locales have at times been somewhat neglected. As the poet Roy Fisher memorably claimed of Birmingham: 'Most of it has never been seen'. The rulers of empire looked outward to the geography of a world they dominated and then back onto their own private domains. Yet the contemporary poets of our post-imperial era, coming from landscapes they and their ancestors have never owned physically but to which they have a strong emotional attachment, stake a different sort of claim – a symbolic claim based on appreciation and attachment rather than on ownership. And the need to make that claim will be reinforced by the restless changes of our own time, uprooting people and altering landscapes. Poetry needs to be a remembering of what *was*, as well as a celebrating of what *is*.

Place, it seems, can be evocative in two ways. First, there is the strong sense – particularly in those parts of the country now regarded as 'picturesque' tourist attractions – of past (often hard) labour embedded in the very landscape. The Lake District, which Wordsworth first suggested should be regarded as a national park, has been tunnelled and quarried for hundreds of years. Joan Lee in 'At Paddy End Copper Mines' captures the difficult but mutual relationship between land and labour in the Coniston Fells:

Men drew themselves into the climate of tunnels,
Went in, knowing their body's stature half of a standing
man,
Went in, some to a deeper, sweatier marriage than farm or
lass could give.

Anna Adams is also a poet intensely responsive to natural beauty who does not forget that the wildest places have been home to communities now lost – through often-violent social upheavals. Registering the scale of human absence on a deserted Hebridean island, she responds directly to 'shrill wren-signals' and 'sighs of pale, bottlegrass-green sea' but then goes further than this lonely beauty to sense the totality of the earth itself:

Here is the axle-tree that holds

The planet in place, and controls the unsleeping traffic.

Second, in a long-settled country such as Britain, there is often a need to make sense of past visions that still haunt us – visions of place that poets and other artists have imbued with special significance. We derive much pleasure from seeing the Pennine Moors through the eyes of the Brontë sisters or from tracing Hardy's footsteps through Wessex. But, as when B. P. Luxton tracks Edward Thomas in 'Adlestrop II', there is still the task of reinterpreting, of seeing anew with our own eyes:

> So *small* a place! One almost began to wonder
> whether it had ever existed except perhaps
> in Edward Thomas's heated imagination
> that day in June, two wars and a world away.

Travelling outside Britain, the Pennine Poets are aware of the need to listen rather than opinionate, not to impose a neocolonial vision but rather to embody the cultural and spiritual diversity of the world. All the poets included here realize that travel is a double-edged experience. The urge to see new places and people is intrinsically positive, a product of that restless desire for exploration which characterizes the human species. And tourism is often economically beneficial to the countries we visit. So far so good. Yet there are reasons why the poetic traveller cannot simply be a collector of the quaint and picturesque. It is all too easy to exploit and objectify those who are less affluent than ourselves. And one way of exploiting people is to see them as simply objects in our viewfinders. It may need an imaginative leap to recognize that the sacred traditions of other cultures include human values neglected in the affluent West. And if we link these two elements together we can see that the traveller will often be in the presence of individuals carrying out rites and traditions that demand respect much more than evocative snapshots.

Indeed a number of The Pennine Poets feel the need to go further, to make their pilgrimage culminate in acceptance of indigenous tradition as having its own independent spiritual value for us. Pauline Kirk in her quietly-attentive 'Postcard of an Indian Ceremony' moves from the vivid but external imagery of 'Dry hills and open plains' to an identification with what she sees. The spectator becomes the participant who at the end shifts naturally into the first-person plural, thus including the reader also:

> We stand waiting our future.

After vividly evoking the otherness of a 'traditional' lifestyle Cal Clothier goes further to remind us that our right to take artistic impressions of other people – who do not have the power to reciprocate – depends on our always accepting that these cultures are not there to serve ours, in however 'aesthetic' and sensitive a manner. The only way we can repay people who fascinate or entrance us by their 'strangeness' is to acknowledge that at the deepest level they are neither exotically strange, nor interestingly other, but equally and validly different. The poetry which enables us to link to the feelings of others is also valuably an art which reveals limitations in our own grasp of their lives. Poetry such as Clothier's 'Morocco: In the High Atlas' compels as much by its sobering revelation of what we do not know as by its embodiment of what we do:

> Though I'd heard a woman in the village
> had died in childbirth
> earlier that day, and though I thought I heard
> the young woman sob,
> still I could not penetrate the art that keeps
> two cultures apart.

The very presence of that evocative plural 'cultures' reminds us that our present, even its holiday moods, is always a product of the past. Or, to put it the other way round, it is only by having a sense of the past that we can understand the present.

Pauline Kirk and Mary Sheepshanks.

Living In History

There is a strong connection between the poetic sense of place and of history, for it is often the former which gives rise to the latter – the poet becoming aware of the earlier lives which have passed on one particular spot. But the emphasis in a historical poem is rather different. The historical sense makes the poet concentrate on the temporal rather than the spatial dimension – as we might say on the vertical rather than the horizontal. When I say 'vertical' I am thinking of the layers of soil through which the archaeologist digs. The poet, like the archaeologist shifting earth, excavates history and language to reveal where we have come from. And of course it is one of the defining characteristics of the historical poem that it can make a large leap in time and space from where poet and reader are actually situated. There are many good reasons for making this leap. At best, we feel a sense of strangeness – 'I am being taken into quite a different world' – along with a sense that some issue of importance to us is being explored. Conflicts that in our present world appear to us in a confused and muddled form can be explored more clearly in a historical context.

A very large-scale and readable example of this is Ian M. Emberson's verse-novel *Pirouette of Earth*. Set in 1936 the work has an epic scale, interweaving three separate plots, which cannot be summarized here. But throughout it shows us how poetry can explore history and, in illuminating history, help us understand the present with its headlines about asylum seekers and refugees. The extract included here, describing the pell-mell retreat of villagers and Republican forces towards Madrid in the Spanish Civil War, throws light on what it meant then and means now to become a refugee. Through the experience of one old man, Pedro, we are brought back to the reality behind a word which, to more fortunate individuals, may seem to belong to the world of newspaper reports from distant countries.

Olga Kenyon makes a leap which is longer historically, but no less vivid and close in human terms, when she speaks through the mouth of a labourer 'Working on the Castlefield Canal 1820'. Again, the poet lends her voice to those who have left no personal records behind them but who created massive structures we sometimes take for granted:

> I was young once – now old at twenty-four.
> Each unlit dawn I walk five miles to work
> To lay rough-hewn blocks along their canal...
>
> It all started here, in our blood and guts.

Cal Clothier, in 'A Vision of Cabeza de Vaca', brings alive yet more distant conflict by the same device of dramatic monologue. He explores issues of human power over other humans through a previously-confident conquistador lost in Mexico for eight years. The speaker is frightened to discover that there is a level where conquistadors and native Americans can be joined by love:

> No longer conquistadors, simply men
> forked naked into the breathless
> Inferno of nature, this new world:
> is this vision of love the ghostly hush
> of vampire lunacy sipping our brains?

There are times when the British (or at least the English) can think of their own country as a place where blessedly little violence has occurred. But it is important to be reminded of the brutal evictions that have taken place on this island. Belatedly, the poet can act as a bard for the lost people of whom only the faintest traces remain, like the 'cleared' Highlanders of Glencalvie in Gerald England's 'Croick Churchyard':

> 'Glencalvie people was in the churchyard
> here, May 24, 1845'

This message, their names, in English,
scratched for ever on the diamond panes,
cries across the years
the fingers that wrote
point at us

They saw their own language dying

Mabel Ferrett has a whole section of her collected poems (*Scathed Earth*) entitled *The Celtic Memory* which evokes an island settled long before the Saxons or the Normans. As a professional historian she is keenly aware that our questions may only receive partial answers from the evidence. So, in 'The Badger Stone':

Did willow, birch and pine
shield once this place
and hide a shrine?

Meanings, guesses, twinned
with blood and stone
tease the wind.

Very often, contemporary women writers feel compelled to explore earlier women's difficult lives. Clearly we encounter again the desire of the poet to give a voice to the voiceless. But such empathy can also provide a way of exploring the more subtle, psychological pressures on modern women. Lesley Quayle imagines the death of 'The Flax-Bleacher's Daughter' who in the poem turns from flesh-and-blood to local legend. Though long-dead, she is still with us:

They found the flax bleacher's daughter
drowned in the mill dam,
naked, cold as swamp,
haltered by the wet swaddle of her hair,
eyes open, blacker than bird cherries...

The flax bleacher's daughter whispers,
stirring the night air, rousing bat and barn owl,
pursues her secret into a niche of light.

Most fundamentally, though, it is family history which
literally tells us where we have come from. Poetry is particularly
suitable for embodying such memories since it is an art form
which is both evocative and physical. In other words, it can
give us both the spirit and the feel of lost times. It can bring
to life those of our ancestors whom traditional history has
erased or gathered as 'the masses'. Such individuals left behind
few written records but have passed on an oral wisdom –
perhaps appreciated belatedly, as in Jean Barker's 'Portrait of
a Foremother':

You told me of an East End childhood
when weary Jews walked from the docks
bearing bundles and exotic speech...
I failed to understand the meaning
but I understood courage –
it was you who taught me to endure.

In 'Nailhouse' Pauline Kirk evokes a family and communal
history in danger of being lost, at the same time as she
acknowledges the reality of the present 'affluent society'. The
world of 'Greatgrandmama' carrying on a long tradition of
necessary female labour with her own mother in the West
Midlands, is vividly evoked for us:

So they sweated together
and sang their hymns. In summer
they would have stripped to the waist.

Yet the poet is not dewy-eyed. Her evocation of the
past is made more telling by her clear-eyed vision of a present
where 'the young favour homes with character':

History is marketable now.
For Greatgrandmama, History was sweat
and a widow's bag of nails.

But this intensely humane poetry with its emotional empathy and social commentary could as well stand in our next section, to which we must now turn.

Lesley and Richard Quayle at Waterstones Bookshop.

Personal > Political

Much of the Pennine Poets' work focuses on doing justice to other people, whether as individuals or in relation to larger social contexts. These larger social contexts may involve politics in its broadest, non-sectarian sense. There is a recognition that in the deepest sense we are all 'world-citizens' now. Like most people of my generation I have intense memories of political 'moments' – from the public gestures of marching against wars to the mundane, necessary discussions in damp meeting-rooms. On occasions, as with the demise of apartheid, I can look back and think I may have made some infinitesimal contribution to its demise along with countless millions of others: more often, it is difficult to see any tangible results of political and social commitments. Yet history tells us that liberty and justice are simple goods for all time, and that they have been sustained and then developed – to include women, Black and Asian communities, people with disabilities – by the struggles of countless individuals who may not have foreseen the effects of their individual stands. For writers this struggle for freedom and justice often takes the form of witnessing to those truths which politicians and the media may choose to ignore. Telling the truth as one sees it can, as Orwell saw, be itself a brave political act. This I think was what attracted me to a Roman poet exiled two thousand years ago. I have concluded this section with my 'Ovid in Exile' in the hope of reminding us that poetry and freedom have always been intertwined. The poet can survive the collapse of empires by a refusal to be cowed, by a commitment to the power of words and the imagination.

Poetry can also relate directly to the political issues of our own era. We have already seen in *Pilgrimages* Cal Clothier's sense of how one-sided our relationships with those outside 'the West' can be. Now, in 'Headhunters', he helps to reveal the power-images and power-words of our imperious and imperial culture:

> And all the while our camera was measuring
> every gesture of hand and eye,
> customs, breasts, delight and shyness – all
> absorbed into the chemical darkness of our film.

Such self-awareness is a necessary prelude to our imagining more equal relationships.

It is not surprising that a whole sub-set of poems in this section concerns war and its terrible accompaniments – most shockingly, genocide. It is interesting to note the role of women poets here as 'war poets'. Anna Taylor chooses to convey the horror of war through an imagined persona. Like Pat Barker in the novel, she shows how women writers can make a distinctive contribution towards our understanding of war's human costs. This is also true of the – if possible – even more disturbing topic of ethnic cleansing and genocide. Anna Adams manages the difficult task of writing something appropriate about the Holocaust by focusing on particular sites of loss and memory. But further commentary seems superfluous here. All one can do is note the memorable phrases by which the poet pays her own homage to the memory of the disappeared. The overgrown graves of Viennese Jews lead her in 'Old Jewish Cemetery within the Viennese Necropolis' to think of the terrible fate which awaited their children:

> for here lie ancestors of smoke –
> the childless folk.

Coming back not only to our own time but also to this relatively fortunate island we find poets facing a very different challenge of finding adequate words. In a society where our affluent consumerism cannot entirely still a sense of unease and anxiety, the poet's role is less dramatic but equally crucial. So we find Jean Barker reflecting in 'Extravaganza' on the you-can-have-it-all culture that can seem pervasive of life on 'this sceptred isle', with its gleaming malls, untidy charity shops and vacated Dome:

I walk through a world
  of discarded clothes,
disintegrating Archer novels
  – and charity for the old –
to a new empty Millennium-
  domed Britain.

Jean Barker's poem brings us back with a bump to the consumer-driven, urban world most of us inhabit. It is not exactly a comforting vision. But then, perhaps, the political and social value of poetry is precisely that it does not offer us comfortable excuses for being the way we are and doing what we do to others and to our environment. Yet this does not mean that the Pennine Poets think we should spend all our time wallowing in agony and guilt about our role in the world. For at the heart of all our lives are our particular, ongoing interactions with our fellow human beings. Arguably our politics, however idealistic, need to be judged against the actual quality of these encounters with the people around us. In different ways both the next two sections of this anthology focus on the quality of our contact with our fellow human-beings.

A World of Neighbours

One thing that may pleasantly surprise readers of this book is how many of the poems concern people and our relationships with them. Sometimes in journalistic accounts modern poetry is seen as over-complex, or as over-concerned with the life and feelings of the poet her/himself. But the work of the Pennine Poets contains a series of vivid portraits of others, with the poet rejoicing in the distinct qualities of individuals. So, Mabel Ferrett reminds us of a continuing, unremarked humanity within our day-to-day, mundane world. Her 'Death of a Neighbour' links suburban reality and a spiritual perspective without denying either:

No! We were never friends; too far apart
  in taste and activity
to touch each other. Yet is it that we stood
  closer than friends can be?

My own poem 'The Shopkeeper' attempts to evoke another of those fellow human-beings whose lives poignantly cross ours in the endless movement of the modern city, imagining his first, lonely experience of the north of England, for him a kind of frontier country after the complex civilization of Pakistan:

Kicking up leaf-drift under sodium lamps,
smelling the Bradford fog and knowing
he is one who has chosen life
in this Northern Frontier land.

Perhaps the poet with the broadest collection of 'Dutch realist' portraits is S.L. Henderson Smith, who often crystallizes his experience as a doctor into vividly-realized evocations of particular hospital patients. The combination of a doctor's eye with poetic skills can produce unexpected results as with his portrait of a 'Long-Stay Case' who turns out to be no object of pity but of awe and a certain admiration:

The hundred things that grace a room
And make it home; he had no need of them
He said, they were encumbrances to reason.

Wordsworth once wrote of our 'little nameless, unregarded acts / Of kindness and of love' and Joyce Thornton's 'Give Us This Day' captures this aspect of our lives. There is a practicality in the woman-weaver baking bread for her tackler (overseer) but there is also a sense of unspoken relationship, of 'tryst', of 'patterns' which are:

cut out, like life, on cards
dropping and rising rhythmically.
Then when knots were tied
she reached inside her pinafore
for the tackler's pains
to keep the thread continuous.

It is the quirky, unexpected individuality of our fellow human-beings, and the ever-surprising dynamics of our relationship with them, which the Pennine Poets evoke. So it is perhaps most appropriate to close this section with Ed Reiss's surreal 'Green as a tomato, green as a banana' with its wonderfully anarchic cast of characters who come:

Out of the door of impossibility

as, perhaps, in our multitudinous eccentricity of individual being, do the rest of us.

K.E.Smith at Waterstones, Leeds.

A Stillness of the Spirit

Religion can invest our lives with meaning and sacredness but can also radically divide us from other human beings. To avoid that divisiveness some of us adopt an inclusive, 'new age spirituality' only to find that we miss some of the certainty of traditional religion. Others, again remain within organized religion yet doubt its more dogmatic side. Poetry, I believe, can get us round this conundrum of modern spiritual life because it is the form of language where the letter becomes the spirit. It can present the most generous, open side of traditional religious faith and can also give solidity and depth to newer, less anchored spiritual pathways. From this calm integration poetry can open us to that 'stillness of the spirit' which begins Mary Sheepshanks's 'Caerhûn Church', a stillness from which we can share in each other's spiritual traditions.

This is not to deny differences or to lack respect for the integrity of different traditions. Certainly, it is true that there are times when I – happening to know whether individual Pennine Poets are Anglicans, Quakers, atheists or whatever – can sense 'where their poems are coming from' in terms of their own affiliation and life-experiences. And I do believe that it is important for everyone to have a distinct spiritual point of departure, whether it is in one of the great faiths or in their own synthesis. Thus I feel in Josie Walsh's poetry a catholic (small 'c') sensibility of a generous kind, one which shows the ability of a Catholic (large 'C') vision to convey the sacramental value of human life. In her 'Waiting' a person is celebrated precisely in the language of nature:

> tall and intricately stamened
> the markings of your hopes and fears
> etched like the foxglove's patterning
> on strong and supple stem, marbled velvet
> green chaliced purple, white, the liturgies of your life
> upright and bending, unbreaking in the breeze,
> a rooted, self-seeded, gracious harvest. Waiting.

Nevertheless I don't think we need to share specific beliefs to appreciate poetry. The power of poetry is in making us empathize, enabling us to draw benefit from areas of human life we may not ourselves have visited. Thus Brian Merrikin Hill has a number of fine poems in which he meditates profoundly on images of the Virgin Mary. We do not have to be practising Catholics (and, most interestingly, the poet himself was not) to derive insight and comfort from these evocations. In 'Notre Dame de Héas' the poet is spiritually strengthened at a shrine but knows he must move on:

> As now, briefly in your dark shrine, Lady of
>   Snows,
> On the way from Sauveterre to Perpignan
> (Or Newcastle on Tyne to life's other city)
> Travelling deviously, finding stone or flower in
>   off-beat valleys,
> I stop to admire your habit of surviving avalanches
> To make here for the faithful a destination none of
>   my journeys reach.

The ecumenical spirituality of Mabel Ferrett, on the other hand, often seems bound up with renewing Biblical and traditional stories. She witnesses afresh where others have witnessed through centuries. The sense of narrative we saw in her history poems is also central to her understanding of religion. Again, one does not have to share orthodox Christian belief to feel how she links common experience to Biblical story. Her task is like that of the sculptor of the scourged Christ on the cross in 'Wood Carving, XV Century':

> Unknown carver,
> whose name I would breathe in prayer, you teach
> that those who love tap the creative springs
> and life begets life, not only through the flesh.
> Through wood and word something strange is passed.

Ian M. Emberson, by contrast, seems more focused on the wonder of the here-and-now. His poetry has the lucidity and glancing freshness of Chinese or Japanese verse. Its moments of spiritual insight are those which could be accommodated either within any religious tradition or outside all of them. To attach theological qualities such as 'good' to beings may be to miss the point of their being at all. In 'The Wind' entities are themselves but not *just* themselves – rather spiritual versions of themselves:

> I am myself,
> the universe itself,

and the wind –
is the wind.

Interestingly, one concern that Emberson shares with Trevor Innes is a literal and spiritual fascination with light. The latter, in the poem 'Moment of Light', focuses on the moment of epiphany, in which the ordinary world becomes magical. The bracketed hesitations make the affirmation of human capacity for spiritual enlightenment all the more poignant and convincing:

> we step aside from our lives
>
> for a moment – as when the spirit leaves the body –
> (though we hardly notice, we cannot find time)
>
> and we say nothing but (where does it come from?)
> become
> graced and limitless ourselves, ourselves a moment
> of light.

There are many moments of light in the poems of this anthology and Andrew Boobier's 'Reality Effect' in particular is suffused with an intense concentration on the act of perception:

> Things-in-themselves waver like steel
> On the quivery human compass.

Boobier's poetry develops one key strain of modern poetry in which the poem is itself a direct exploration of being-in-the-world. In such poetry of creative process it seems impossible to separate the mundane and the spiritual. Yet however fulfilling this world of 'things-in-themselves' may be, we also need poetry which deals with the last things of life, and not least with our individual mortality. Robert Williams in 'snow-line' begins a profound exploration of the spiritual journey with a statement at once strange and familiar:

> Death is the solitary visitor whose
> name you know.

Poetry such as that of Robert Williams or Brian Merrikin Hill may go into and out of the fashion of a decade but it will endure because it speaks of these ultimate truths that we cannot avoid. Ultimately, more even than 'the pursuit of happiness', we need the assurance that our lives are meaningful and valid.

**Josie Walsh, Mabel Ferrett and Christine England
at Pennine Poets meeting.**

The Natural World

Inseparable from this search for larger meaning is the question of the relationship between the human and the non-human – between ourselves and all that we call 'nature'. Indeed, to British readers at least, the link between poetry and nature seems, in a word, natural. Even those who do not care a great deal for poetry may know by heart lines such as 'I wandered lonely as a cloud' or 'Season of mists and mellow fruitfulness'. But the Pennine Poets are living two hundred years after Wordsworth and Keats so it should not surprise us if they see nature, as well as the rest of life, somewhat differently. For one thing, landscape is now seen as having its own human history written into and on it, as bearing the marks of human intervention. This can give rise to a sense of both transience and endurance as in Clare Chapman's 'Terraces':

> The all-devouring grave of constant earth
> Is marked with terraces,
> With Iron-Age ridges on the down, the mound
> And strong-hold fields' perimeter.

This fusion of human interventions and landscape reminds us that nature and human culture have always been interacting with each other.

Nevertheless, a more purely 'green' perspective remains vital to the Pennine Poets. Each particular entity in nature is seen to have its own unique value – independently of its use or otherwise for us. Poetry can be very good at pinpointing those places and creatures that are at once vulnerable and symbolic of life's power of renewal. This is vividly brought home by a poem such as John Walker's 'Eggs':

The egg clutch grabbed at my heart,
oh,
laid on the ground in a litter of brown bracken
                              stalks and dried leaves,
visible,
but enough camouflaged for a foot to tread on,
full, rounded treasures,
nestled, clustered,
each one touching another,
complete in itself.

The special, spiritual value which the Romantics attached to nature is still felt but in altered ways. We find poets who meditate intensely on particular plants or animals. Chris Bousfield presents us with 'The Hare', a creature which is very real, 'a fierce and cunning mother' but also a stark, emblematic presence:

But I have two faces, two dances
to wrong-foot the gods, naked as emperors.
I scurry, a shadow, carrying wild grasses
to those they would see die.

It is precisely where the human-made dominates that the necessity of nature to our spiritual well-being becomes most pressing. S.L. Henderson Smith's 'Hospital Starlings' in the middle of an unremarkable courtyard have an enhanced value:

There is a courtyard even so within –
A solitary tree left idle has a task
Incongruous in its benign simplicity –
To shelter starlings, silly, restless specks
Of black and purple; each gathering dusk
They chatter in language from another world
Bring music from the fields, the woods
To vitalise our cold modernity.

There is a special value in such close, loving attention in a world which is often hurried and inattentive to its surroundings. Mary Sheepshanks is a poet whose anxious questioning can be stilled by the God of small things, as in the sudden illumination of 'Kingfisher Days':

> An electric flash of unexplained delight
> – a kingfisher moment – streaked across my day
> like blue-green rockets torched on bonfire night.
> Where did it come from? Why? I cannot say.

A broader perspective on bird-flight is found in Ian M. Emberson's 'Rook Flight at Evening Over Farnley Moor', where the emphasis is on energy, process and movement in nature:

> suddenly the far
> ocean of dusk with rook-cawed rioting rings,
> as birds on birds, with clashing ebony cry,
> eclipse that flamed fantasia of sky.

Above all, there is a strong sense that the human world does not exist in contradistinction to nature but as a distinctive part of it – a distinctive part not least because it is only we on earth who can articulate nature to itself in words and images. Gordon H. Dyson, in 'A Visit to Sète' hears:

> A current of song wordless and yet
> Full of absolute meaning, absolute meaning,
> The absolute music of the sea.

So, paradoxically, the very existence of 'nature poetry' leads us to reflect on the power of words to capture what lies beyond words. Just why and how have poetry and the other arts this ability to capture and make coherent the 'blooming, buzzing confusion' of the world around us?

Mabel Ferrett, Albert Thornton and Joyce Thornton launching
Pennine Twenty-Five, October 1991. Reprinted by kind permission
of the *Spenborough Guardian*.

Art, Craft and Labour

The Pennine Poets have taken a wide interest in the making of literature and the other arts, but this interest should not be seen as a precious or rarefied one. It is in any case often the 'human angle' of artist and works of art which attracts the poets, so that even a poem about another poet turns out to be about qualities of humanity, as in Fred Schofield's 'For William Carlos Williams 1883-1963'.

> your words
> point
> to the ancient journey
>
> we've all made to survive
> time and make
> our lives.

For another, the arts are seen as having intimate connections with all other kinds of human labour. This is a point worth dwelling on. It recalls that poetry itself is creative labour and the poet, as old Scots had it, a maker (*makar*), someone who crafts verse as others turn chair-legs or design computer programs. In Jim Kempster's 'Arabesque' the poem appears to be about ballet-dancing but in a humorous, thought-provoking twist, turns out to be also about the very process of writing the poem itself. In fact all the makers featured in this anthology have a healthy admiration for the sheer range of skills involved in labour by hand and brain. Nicholas Bielby in 'the Smithy at Haworth' values the blacksmith for having abilities he, doubtless like most of his readers, could not match:

> He's forged his freedom, having made
> His craft his trade

and Mary Sheepshanks mourns the 'Death of a Craftsman':

> To watch him carve a chair,
> Mend clocks or paint a room
> Was to feel all the rhymes and metres
> Flowing right.

And who is to deny that the intense, organized efforts of sport and the passionate involvement of thousands in sporting success or failure are not also fit subjects for the poet's admiration? Those who doubt this should at least test their intuitions against John Cook's vivid football poem 'All for a Point'.

Of course it should not surprise us that poets show a particular interest in the parallel but different experience of practitioners across the whole range of the arts. Gerald England shows us how words can take off from the flow of music and express some of its inner meaning in his 'Hindemith: Concerto for Organ, 1962':

> the chords in the air,
> not yet cut
> nor yet surmised
> No awareness of scissors.

But from all the wide range of cultural influences on the Pennine Poets two very different ones are conspicuous. The first main cultural influence, that of painting, is not surprising when we consider that several of the Pennine Poets are as committed to the visual arts as they are to poetry. But again, the interest is more universal. Paintings are valued for their ability to encapsulate the essence of human interactions beyond particular images.

The painting becomes an emblem of the human condition. Sometimes the poet wishes to draw attention to the way the image carries a universal significance in a way that words can usefully point to, but no more. For Pauline Kirk 'The Night Café: Vincent Van Gogh, 1888' is a commonly-experienced yet terrifying purgatory many will know in other guises:

> Most of us have passed a night here,
>
> though in other cities, other times.

A very different approach to Van Gogh can be found in Catherine Emberson's 'Palette' which envisages the painter's most vivid images as 'his soul laid bare'. Elsewhere, the appeal of painting for the Pennine Poets seems to be its open, suggestive quality. It is fascinating to see how, totally independently, Anna Adams and Julia Deakin meditate on Van Eyck's *Betrothal of the Arnolfini*. Both render the rich colouring and formal complexity of the painting yet acknowledge the mysteriousness of the man and woman who look out at us. As Julia Deakin concludes 'their hearts are colours/we can only guess'.

More generally, because of the visible labour of painting and the painter's intense relationship with a living model the artist can seem to embody the stress and strain of all the arts. The very act of painting can often be for the writer the most vivid and tangible type of the creative enterprise itself. In 'Edvard Munch Sets Up His Easel' Clare Chapman captures the feverish relationship between the artist and his ailing sister-model:

> Scrape, scrape for the bone under that skin
> Trace line by line the courses fever takes
> You flat ground show dimensions of the wraith.

The other main cultural influence on the work of the Pennine Poets is much more specific: the lives and work of the Brontës. In a Yorkshire context this might not seem surprising but there are deeper affiliations than those of shared places. Both the commitment to their art and their tragic struggles have produced awe and empowerment. At least five of the poets in this volume have written 'Brontë poems'. By no means all are included here but those that are, link biographical detail with imaginative vision.

In 'Patrick at Hartshead', Mabel Ferrett displays her usual unobtrusive skill in merging historical knowledge and sympathetic human drama. She imagines Patrick Brontë as curate of Hartshead, during the Napoleonic Wars sharing 'a silence of secrets' over a clandestine Luddite burial in the churchyard. Ian M. Emberson's 'Life's Lone Wilderness' brings alive for us the situation of Charlotte Brontë as she finished *Shirley* after the deaths of her brother and sisters. The poet unobtrusively links the three 'narratives' of nature, art and life:

She watches from that lonely house
the narrative of sky –
the cirrus twisting in the wind
beyond the grouse's cry –

The poem satisfies because it at once conveys to us something special and remarkable about Charlotte's vision and yet makes her the repository of basic feelings we have all shared. And it intrigues because it hints at our age-old yearning for the sight of things invisible and spiritual behind entities visible and material, however beautiful the latter may be. Yet it is the poet's insertion of that simple adjective 'lonely' that anchors his vision of Charlotte Bronte and reminds us that poetry, however exalted and visionary, always starts from and returns to, the world of human relationships.

Clare Chapman.

What Will Survive of Us

Within the broad circle of our relationships with the people we meet is embedded a tighter, more intense circle of feeling – that of our most intimate relationships with partners, parents and children. These are areas which poetry has made its own through the ages and at all levels – from the love poetry of John Donne to the obituaries in our local newspapers – and there is no sign that more modern media are about to usurp this role. Indeed, one could argue that as communication speeds up it is only poetry that can slow and deepen words so as to do justice to our most intimate feelings. Nevertheless, the poetry that is written around these relationships is very different from that with which, say, the Victorians surrounded the family. Indeed, if we wanted a single 'defence' of contemporary poetry it might be that our intimate relationships have been changed radically in the last century and that we need our poets to help us map those changes.

Nowhere are these changes more apparent than in poems about parenting, where we are often seeking the words which can describe relationships very different from those of the past. Judith Bolland's poetry, for example, captures the subtle and changing relationship between older and younger sibling, blending an authentic note of experience with unobtrusively skilful word-choices so that what she describes in 'At Thanksgiving' seems at once universal and familiar:

> Frail fledgeling, I claimed you.
> And you thrived, grew,
> outstripped us all.

Poetry is often at its best when it deals with those aspects of our lives that seem too close, too particular to us, to be the subject of art. So, along with acknowledging the precious, fragile gift of children, the Pennine Poets meditate on relationships with parents or their surrogates. Above all, what relationships demand of us is emotional honesty and specific ways of going forward. Chris Bousfield in her sequence 'Mother' captures this aspect in words that subtly align the forms of poetry with those of intimate relationships:

> I'm sorry. We're not supposed to rhyme
> with each other, you and me; best work
> at maintaining our boundaries.
> Which means edges.

Joan Lee recalls her own mother in 'Poem for Brett'. Only now it is the magical power of poetry to bring the dead back to life that is highlighted:

> Proudly you are torn from me now, but a scent remains.
> Your old age stumbled up the sloping hill for a posy.

At their best the Pennine Poets cut through both Victorian piety about the family and its converse, the Larkinesque blame of our ills on 'mum and dad'. A poem such as Albert Thornton's 'Spoiled Child' manages to be about enduring gratitude *and* life-long emotional burdens at the same time – as its perfectly-judged, ambiguous title suggests.

Lastly in this section – but by no means leastly – the Pennine Poets contribute their tribute to the oldest human theme of poetry, that of 'love and song'. The relationships between lovers remain – or perhaps become even more of – a mystery as technocracy advances. It is poetry rather than therapy or science which can best encapsulate the joys and pains bound up in that mystery. The loss of love can be given its proper weight and dignity in poetry. The stone that Gordon H. Dyson cuts through to in 'Au Saint Severin' seems to be his bereft self:

> I meet, for example, the stone
> So snugly embedded in the peach I cut
> In remembrance of you.

We have already seen poignant separation and difference captured in a different way by Linda Marshall in 'Incompatible' where gifts of rainbows and stars can turn to pain because 'rainbows and stars/ Are like day and night'. Again, in her evocative miniature novel 'French Chalk' Joyce Thornton hints at a whole world of passion which could only be briefly and silently expressed in one magical, chance encounter. But there is also love's gratitude and fulfilment. Anna Taylor's love poems from the long *Fausta* Sequence inhabit a more open-ended world. Her lovers on the moorland with 'dreams like slippery births' at once evoke the Brontë novels yet capture a peculiarly modern sensibility. They are contradictory, unfinished, modern people:

> Our steps sliding backwards
> our rickety pasts.

Again, there is an interesting contrast to be made between the shifting directness of Anna Taylor's love poetry and the witty poignancy of Ed Reiss's equally contemporary, more allusive idiom. But it seems appropriate to close this section of love poetry on more traditional, though still recognizably modern, notes. The poetry of Howard Frost contains a series of intense love-poems, often in sonnet form. If at times a poem such as 'To a Pair of Blue Eyes', evokes the troubadour poetry of the past, it also has a note of vulnerability and confessed need which is peculiarly of our own time, as the poet yearns not to be among 'all the lonely people' but to be held and fulfilled:

> Oh you whose eyes are sapphire swords of light
> That flash to kill, or glance to wound a soul.
> Lend me your blade and make of me your knight,
> Take me into your arms and make me whole.

Finally, we encounter a wholly organic vision of love, which sees it as fluidly entwined with our relationship to the natural. Pat Borthwick's 'Vertebrae' displays her capacity to evoke the human and the non-human simultaneously, to convey – in a way that logic rules out – that they are at once utterly different yet part of the same totality. She has been describing nature as full of sensuous movement and 'lusting' energy. When in the last line she suddenly switches to the world of two human lovers there is an initial shock. Then the reader sees how all the life-celebrating imagery that has gone before can also be applied to the now-calm couple:

My love, our quiet bones are all these.

Howard Frost at Oakwell Hall.

Voices on the Page

Yet such a sense of completeness is in the end only achievable through the distinct rhythm and pitch of the individual poet, of the voice's imprint on the page. At first we may only be aware of a general 'feel' which is satisfying but on returning to the poems we are aware of that specific voice, affecting our response as much as the larger issues raised. So it is fitting, as we approach the end of our study of the Pennine Poets, that we listen more holistically to a few of the individual voices we have already encountered.

As W.H. Auden wrote, in *September 1, 1939*, 'All I have is a voice…' The distinctive quality of an individual poet's voice may be more difficult to define than his or her fund of imagery or metrical skill but it is no less real. And this is not just a matter of having heard a particular poet read their work out loud, memorable and invaluable though that can be. The distinctive voice is just as much there in the words read silently on the page. Think of a line of poetry such as 'Do not go gentle into that good night' or 'What will survive of us is love' and you hear the inner voice of Dylan Thomas or Philip Larkin. So also with the Pennine Poets.

There is a special intensification of our awareness when we hear a known voice exploring new areas of experience, perhaps changing in timbre and pitch but remaining recognizably the same voice. So it is important that in doing justice to the thematic range of the Pennine Poets as a group, we do not lose touch with the integrity and wholeness of their individual voices. We cannot of course even attempt this for several dozen very different poets but, however briefly, let me try and capture the voices of just five currently active Pennine Poets – Linda Marshall, Josie Walsh, Ed Reiss, Julia Deakin and Nicholas Bielby.

The first of these, Linda Marshall, is a good example of a poet with an unmistakeable idiom of her own who yet manages to cover a wide range of poetic registers. For one thing she is a successful performance poet as well as a book and magazine one – so she is well-aware of writing certain poems for the page and others much more explicitly for reading out loud. But more subtly, she can move from humour to sadness in one poem and then from sadness to humour in another. Her poetry gets us away from the identification of solemnity with seriousness. Yet its light tone and swift movement should not be mistaken for frivolity. Rather, she shows us how the profound moments come out of the daily detail. For me her work evokes the vision of the Jewish theologian Martin Buber with his emphasis on the centrality of the 'I-Thou' relationship at the heart of the human world. An uneasy tea 'At Betty's' [café] can suddenly flow into something quite different:

> Sitting at a tangent, deeply distracted;
> The silence between us, jarring
> In the murmur of voices, mix of laughter;
> The high romantic windows looking out
> On huge snowflakes, swirling as if shaken –
> But it is mid-May; the flurry is white
> Cherry blossoms skidding on a cool wind
> That signals change. We begin to talk...

Josie Walsh is a very different poet, reminding us that if we try to talk about 'women's poetry' as a single entity we may end up being reductive. (One could certainly argue that contemporary women poets share a capacity to avoid dogma and to follow E.M. Forster's advice: 'only connect....' But beyond that, women poets today are simply too numerous and too variously talented to be generalized about). Walsh's meditative quality and sacramental language contrast strongly with the dramatic framework of Linda Marshall's poetry. For a non-Catholic reader her work has the great virtue of making available a long-standing tradition, one of respecting and valuing what Hopkins called the 'inscape' of the individual life. This tradition sees the creative arts as the means of celebrating that union between the temporal and the eternal.

It is a vision which this reader at least finds hugely supportive in the modern world: Walsh's work can deal equally well with the detritus of our urban-rural borderlands or with carved marble in a sculptor's studio. Like Hopkins, she sees the special value of each separate item in the world, though her style is quite different – the kind of poetic voice like that of Robert Frost or Edward Thomas that seems as much overheard as heard, and which is all the more effective for insinuating itself into our minds without our being totally conscious of its effect on us. When she writes in 'October' that 'The ghosts are pressing again' her words sound uncannily like the reader's own private thoughts.

We might characterize Ed Reiss as a poet who cannot easily be characterized, as a writer who always surprises us. But this – although validly pointing to the unexpected twists of his work – could be misleading. There is never any clever smoke-and-mirrors air to his poetry, never any sense of speaking to a literary coterie. Rather he works by avoiding the clichéd route which the reader might be inclined to follow. But after we have been wrong-footed, pushed at a door which was already open, felt the surprise of his work, we equally feel its rightness – and have the strong sense that 'all' he has done is to follow the words and meanings where they lead. Needless to say that 'all' is not something most of us could hope to replicate. It is peculiar to the poet and then, seemingly, logical for the rest of us.

There is that indefinable openness to his work – a sense that the poem is exploring new territory even as it develops – which has been a great virtue of American poetry in the last century: it manages to be profoundly democratic and artistically demanding at the same time. Ed Reiss's poetry seems to combine British wit with American directness in a truly creative union. In 'Picture Postcards' he both shows his subtle way with the clichés that we use to keep our lives flowing, and creates from his eccentric collector a credible lover of humanity:

Most of all he liked the jokes,
however lame. Of picturesque
thatched cottages – *hovels.*
Tell the lads in Planning:
Knock 'em down. Or this
from Sandringham: *popped in on E*
and P, who send their kind regards.

Julia Deakin's is also a difficult voice to classify – that is, if we make the mistake of wanting to classify poets. There is an unusually broad spectrum of tone, from sharp-edged challenge to compassionate reflection, in her poetry. She can move from well-crafted, compressed 'short stories' in verse to more subtle and allusive narratives. Looking through her work one is struck by the ease with which she finds the appropriate form for her poems. If it is a regular form she needs, so be it, if it is a freer form then that too will be used, though never without artistic discipline. It is true that her work does share a confidence and inventiveness that characterize the best of her generation of British women poets – poets who came to maturity in the last decades of the twentieth century. In her case this fearlessness enables her to deal particularly well with those disturbing-embarrassing-poignant memories of 'ordinary' (which usually means extraordinary) family life that haunt so many of us. A poem such as *'Jump!'* beginning:

I am a child planted on a path which curves away

captures a present pain, but the transparency of language and calm unfolding put the experience in a larger context. Memory and the evocation of loss play a big part in her poetry but so also do 'secret narratives' that set the reader on creative detective work. Her poetry, with its linguistic alertness and pointed imagery, reminds us that poetry can be a way not just of recalling our experience but also of filling out and recreating our past lives.

Nicholas Bielby.

Our final voice is that of Nicholas Bielby. But this time, instead of characterizing his whole poetic output, let us for a change focus on a single sonnet, his 'In Memory of William Coleman, Aged Two' which for me shows poetry's ability to crystallize deep feeling on a difficult topic – the death of a child. The poem begins, beautifully but deceptively, with a natural image which does not seem to relate immediately to the announced subject. But the fall of the cherry blossom, making 'an autumn-out-of-season' and sifting 'its random petals down the air', prepares us gently but firmly for the entry of the main theme. This, when it emerges in the fifth line, is stark and unvarnished. It would not be right to dress up the child's death in fine words:

> William is dead, who once held both hands out
> to grasp life like a gift or flower.

Unobtrusively, the poem moves on to address the boy's parents directly, stressing the completeness and adequacy of the love they gave their child, before ending its first eight lines (the octet) with a poignant might- have- been. If love were indeed omnipotent then they 'who gave him life, would hold him still'.

The sonnet's last six lines (or sestet) move us on to the present and the future, acknowledging the totality of loss but also hinting how time can transmute (not deny or destroy) the pain of grief. That change can and does happen even to the bereaved is subtly conveyed in the half-rhymes of these last lines. Before, all the rhymes in the poem had been perfect but now we have the sequence 'until – feel – pearl' which gives a more dynamic, open-ended feeling to this last section. The poet can now work his way through to a tentatively positive conclusion. Through a painful transformation:

> what you feel
> of grief and loss becomes a gift: as if
> the holding had itself become a pearl.

As with other Nicholas Bielby poems, 'In Memory' shows how the conscious art of the poet does not detract from but at once intensifies and shapes life's most basic feelings. It is hard to imagine a more 'difficult' or painful subject but the poem does what our ordinary words cannot do. It shares and respects the unique grief of losing a child but also sets it in a larger, positive pattern of love's redemptive power.

All of these poets remind us of poetry's unique capacity to show us the world we share through the revealing lens of a creative temperament, distinct in each case but very much sharing the same world as the rest of us. In an age when it is easy to be 'taken over' by the multiplicity of media and computer images, the range of material goods and brand-names, they remind us that everything in our world exists to be re-seen and re-evaluated by each individual. But like good actors on the stage these poets are also aware that being 'naturally themselves' requires a sense of significant form and a mastery of communicative techniques – techniques used with a subtlety that makes us forget technique completely and see all as 'natural', giving us the sense that we share for a time in another's world which also becomes our own world.

What then?

Long continuance of the Pennine Poets has led to a specific, and I believe, valuable sense of identity and purpose. But the group is not static and there has never been one 'in-crowd'. New members quickly establish their presence alongside the older ones. Some may come for a short time only – and if they move away and on to other groups or affiliations then that is surely natural and healthy for them. (I have never heard such individuals say negative things about their time with the Pennine Poets – quite the opposite). Others will stay for years, decades even, not out of inertia but because each time there are fresh criticisms and insights to take home and learn from. Naturally, there have been sad losses of older members over the years but it is curious how the empty places are unobtrusively filled by new generations of poets. These new voices should not be thought of as 'fitting in' to the workshops and readings in some rather passive, limiting way. Rather they are catalysts who alter the feel of the whole group in subtle ways.

Groups, like individuals, have their limitations as well as their strengths – or should one say that their limits are precisely the outward edges of their strengths? I will leave the reader to fill in those types or areas of poetry which the Pennine Poets have not practised. Doubtless there are quite a few, for the world of poetry certainly has more mansions than any one group could ever fill. Again, each individual reader will bring to this anthology his or her own presuppositions about what poetry is or should be. Anyone who believes poetry should avoid politics, religion or other contentious issues altogether and remain a thing apart will be liable to feel disappointment with this collection. So also will anyone who thinks that poetry should be direct propaganda for a cause or a dedicated following of fashion. Yet I would guess that most of those who open this book will share my basic premises: that on the one hand the subject-matter of poetry is the whole of our life and not just a part of it, and on the other that socially-committed art works best when politics is only one level of its multi-layered existence.

Here, then, is a group of poets who combine dedication to their 'craft or sullen art' with a shared sense of being in the same world as their parents, partners, children, readers and fellow-citizens of a fragile earth. If there is a shared dedication to the 'well-made poem' this does not make for uniformity. I would imagine that, if early pioneers of the Pennine Poets such as Joan Lee or Stephen Henderson Smith could return, they might at first find the poetry of Ed Reiss or of Linda Marshall a little startling. But I believe they would also find strong continuities of theme and concern, and above all a belief in the enduring significance of what Jon Silkin has characterized as 'the poetry of the committed individual'. It does not look to me as if the world will soon be able to dispense with such alert and vivid witnesses to its condition.

But now, rather than my further asserting the value of the Pennine Poets' work in this commentary, it is time to turn to the poetry itself. The poets and their work will certainly make a much more powerful claim for themselves than my overview ever could. Let one of their number, the late Brian Merrikin Hill – believer in the eternal feminine and long-time champion of poetry through his editing of *Pennine Platform* magazine – have the last word here. For this often profound writer reminds us that the reason why poetry can be demanding is that it seeks to uncover a simplicity which our routines of daily living have concealed. His brief poem 'Truth' confirms that poetry still enables us to focus on the great, shared commonplaces of our lives, to find them once more fresh and individual and to explore them fully, to 'know the place for the first time':

> Ultimately there is truth only in simple statements:
> in Autumn the leaves fall; I love you; we shall die.
> Ultimately there is comfort only in simple actions:
> the impulsive caress, laughter, the urge to cry.

K.E. SMITH
Kirkheaton
Autumn 2004 – Summer 2006

**Pennine Poets at the launch of Spirit and Emotion, Cleckheaton
Library, 2006
from back l. to r.: Lesley Quayle, Josie Walsh,
Linda Marshall (hidden), Andrew Boobier,
Julia Deakin, Nicholas Bielby, John Cook, Joyce Thornton,
Anna Taylor, Catherine Emberson, Ian M. Emberson,
Pauline Kirk, Mabel Ferrett, K.E.Smith.**

THE POEMS

—

INDEX OF POETS

YORKSHIRES OF THE MIND

DRIVING HOME ON A MOOR

High up and cold we drove across you
On a B road twisting like a gymnast's ribbon.
Isolate houses were alert to villains.
Their Halogen lamps flared silently,
Their alarms looked us over, winked,
Electric islands repelled us
With their barking jangles.

So we scurried over you,
No illumination but headlights
Trapping luminous eyebulbs,
Hypnotizing rabbity nerves
Until we slowed, graciously,
Let them hop into the hedge.

Then you opened up.
Sky fell about us and a thin breeze.
The moon was low. It was not Poetic.
It was Astronomic, pitted with Death Valleys.
It is the car's movement that creates the wind,
Compounds of lead and carbon buckle grass
But over us a war, conflict of cloud,
A monarch swirling a cape,
A tumbling of wool,
Our voices wither under this boiling.

Clare Chapman

HUMBER BRIDGE

Though sheltered from the starless night
by ingle-arch where fire burns
and books are read and gossip shared,
he finishes with talk and turns
away from the assuaging light
to the blind bay-window's void.

He senses threat of wind and sea.
The bell-note from the current's knock,
up-estuary, invades the town.
Landlubbers, too, absorb the shock,
briefly, of that immensity
of flood-tide and the bridge's girth.

Under the arch the waters boil
in runnels, deep where force meets force,
confronting of the ocean surge
with river's downward thrusting course,
eternal warring, surf and soil;
the bridge that for a span rides both...

Next morning, as the sparkling sea
cancels the carnage of the night,
he walks beside the estuary
marking the seagulls' dipping flight,
slide and divide of treachery,
love and despair, his flesh the bridge.

Mabel Ferrett

THAT DAY

Gillamoor looked great that day,
the done-heather brown over the hillside,
bare trees exposing the moor to view
Surprise View still surprises
by its continuing ability to do so
The low November sun sought out
the shades as numerous as the
lights of brown in your hair.
That day I was not hurtling
down the motorway to meet you
I was cutting over the moors
to the North East's coast
It wasn't you I was meeting that day
but you'd have enjoyed the drive
and the subsequent lunch on the pier
by the sea

I did

Gerald England

SPURN HEAD

This was a place of dream, a source of light.
From a beach far south a child saw a faery tower
beyond an enchanted lake
(the lake was a mirage of sea-wet sand
that merged with a muddy estuary); by night
to that boy's dark road winding through reeded land
for many a lonely hour
it flashed a rhythmic message he mistook.

He confused it in legend. It aimed to warn, as a point
of reference to establish where one was,
threading a deceptive world
of mist on waves whose currents wound through sand
to reach safe havens. It survived the brunt
of sea biting or mining fragile land,
being founded to impose
a stable order where the shifty whored with the wild.

For the boy it did not achieve this, but the dream
(held sixty years) brings the child's heart here to gauge
the substance of the myth:
unfixed yet lasting this marram-bound, thorn-bushed sand;
gaunt skeletal groynes are statues carved by storm
to the transmigration of the soul of land;
bright pebbles at the water's edge
mix a whole island's rocks – wold, sill, peak, strath.

Quartz, basalt, jasper, agate, porphyry, chalk,
granite, oolite, flint, conglomerate, jet,
and sea-lathed banded stones
fringe this heroic spur of glistening sand,
jewelling its torment; pieces of ruined brick
are polished as brooch or necklace for this land
and the fossil ammonite
witnesses formal triumph, given crystal bones.

A place of dream found true, a source of light,
a guide, not visionary comfort, pier
for hardened pilots primed
with knowledge of the paths of sea and sand.
Earth charts how the human metaphor thwarts defeat:
waves twist and wrench the vertebrae of this land
but rhythms of the lanterned tower
join them to channels where the same tides glide becalmed.

Brian Merrikin Hill

from HORCUM

The Hole, they had concurred in, was not Natural.
The Giant Weadda, or Wade
scooped it out of Blackamoor when it occurred
that his wife, the original Hilda,
made off towards Whitby great strides, but slow.
He flung what had been the Hole at her
and I suppose he missed: the pile
we now call Blakey Topping represents
the missile: eastward about a mile
it rests. And, with the Hole, wants explanation
when you walk all day within sight of them.

Here where the wind has carved its permanent way
and the gripp-plough is sending down by the becks
the peatworld of the moorlands into the dale
the Hole that we are in dies in flecks.

                There are trees, so old and bare
                they do not hold the breeze:
                leaftime here and sere
                are the same season to these.

The redshank doesn't ask for echoes here
as the curlew requires of the hill
there's hardly space for the twisting snipe to shear
his drumroll between the closing cliffs.

A place for the urgency of echoes,
the agency of rock.

The stars cannot keep their dancing circle:
they fall into the surrounding moor
not run to the horizon.

The hole had produced 'High Horcum' of itself
the farm they lived in was as of the place
as if one landslip, neater than the rest
had proceeded whole to the lowest part of the bowl
by the beck, scattered loose stones for a pinfold
for the sheep, and come to rest the right-way up
and grown its blocks together
mortar its shale and kept to scale:
a reptile thing, cold-blooded and square-ended
as Horcum seasons were: the whole alive, or nothing.

Colin Simms

'Bridestone above Todmorden', Ian M. Emberson.

BEYOND LEATHLEY

This is not Top Withens, nor any such literary place,
but an unnamed farm that raised a stubborn face
towards sullen land and obstinate fields.

Now lintels hewn by giants frame a broken sky;
balance door shafts in Georgian symmetry.
A courtyard shines through grass –

we walk it down a crystal afternoon.
Pheasants rasp like rusty gates, and a shred of moon
surprises. Slowly the land becomes softer.

Celandines splash light; a milky way of wood aven
glows beside a stream. Yet even in this quiet haven
winter debris strews the scene. Branches

breed monsters; whole trees lie, roots clamped
in clay. Two hundred years of growth ended
in one February storm, yet today that same wind

offers life. I gulp its gift, forgetting the afternoons
lost to darkness, the eternity of mud-soaked March.
Like the celandines I turn towards the sun, and open.

Pauline Kirk

MALHAM COVE

Cream curve
of the sealess sea cliffs
of the sealess cove,
where houseless martins gull-glide
the green green waves,
and hawthorn flowers
and fingering leaves of ash
crash-cry upon its limestone precipice.

Ivy is insolent
to turn those furthest sides
into a semblance of a man-made fort,
but does not quite
dare be invasive of that central sweep
where the recessing viaduct of the rocks
shows how the water once
spat spume and thundered.

Relaxed
under the gaze
of sentimental eyes
it holds the casket of a mystery –
deeper than the drip-worn grykes
and the river's vein below,
and older than the age of ice.

Ian M. Emberson

ON MAGNUM MOOR

A white horse
Flies across
The black torn moor
And disappears
Into a cloud
of grey mist
That swirls up
Into this
Mysterious night,
A creaking wind
Looks for a
Silent house
As the rain
Sweeps down
And the streams
Rush and roar
Their way down
Endless ravines
A crescent moon
Blinks in between
Disturbed clouds
A storm awaits
Its turn to twist
The slumber of the
Sleeping child,
The stars are lost
Hidden in jewel boxes
Waiting for another
Clear moonlit night
To sing their silent song.

Laurie Stead

SCARFACE

(view from Flockton Moor)

This landscape is hand-made – an artefact
hacked up and stitched together bit by bit:
each slap of mortar, brick and lick of pointing,
plumb-lined chimney stack, each post, each tile,
once chosen from the pile, eclipsed the world
just long enough, until aligned and set in place,
to hold some farm hand's breath an instant,
critically.

That row of trees each had their moment, too
as saplings, chosen, planted, spaced and watered in;
again, a held breath checking the earth's axis
momentarily. Even the hollows on that hillside
trace the lines of ancient mine shafts, worked out
blow by blow, inch by breathless inch –
which only the hands of wind and rain
now rearrange.

Julia Deakin

LISTER'S MILL

From Bolton Junction, the valley's other side,
it looks impressive. Your eye is taken by
the chimney, copied from a campanile
in Venice, mecca of wealth and trade,
as Bradford in its day could claim to be.
This distant view gives only the building's strength,
its square Victorian lines and scale.
Against a clouded sky it stands stark proud.

A great central tower, its roof like a strange
and steep-angled hat, bisects the long lines.
Below and to the right Manningham Park
and Heaton greenspace frame it. Miles westward,
just in view, slimmer towers hold up great blades,
clean new turbines gleaning the moorland winds.

                                        John Cook

PEN Y GHENT

Hills of the border, where the bare fells end
and surge up to this massy sphinx of black grit
that lies along the valley's horizons; head raised
to gaze, had it eyes, across the flattened land.

In mist an enigma; a cold force that will emerge,
loom like a shadow above streamlet's leak
or murk of thorn; the droplets coalesce, darkness,
a whisper, a shape that expands like a spreading bruise.

The face is raw, wet rock that frosts have battered
and shaled. In cracks saxifrage push delicate flowers
above tough leaves, tiny, purple in bright April light
– tatters of royal, priestly gown that sparkle like blood.

                                        Colin Speakman

LUMB LANE, BRADFORD

At noon the street coaxed men
and dusky children around the Mosque,
women, peering through muslined air,
the frangibility of veils with no clear synthesis of faces,
black irises and arched brows, unplucked.
Dark, impenetrable, unfurtive eyes.

Memory tossed up old conspiracies
of a twilight alley where,
curious to see,
I had lingered among besieged mansions,
shuttered, un-slated, burned and martyred,
alone with the nocturnal smells
which thickened the breath of the night
like cheap liquor.

A cat regarded me
with its green, glass eyes,
flattened itself along the gutter
to watch a woman lit by an open door.
Light roosted among peroxide curls,
crept down a thin, white neck to scribe her breasts.
She smoothed her hair,
shivered in the piercing wind,
cold bones wrapped up like a sack of knives.

Today, a dry wing of air stretches across the pavement,
stirs the embers of burnt out buildings;
ordinary people, clutching their gods,
step out on the unremarked path
from prayers to broken promises.

Lesley Quayle

HUDDERSFIELD

For Michael Kruszynski,
Polish composer

Huddersfield survives for me
not on a map of coloured inks
but in the scribbled nerveways of my brain,
as indestructible as Pennine water
or the wintered silhouette of Scapegoat Hill.

There is the town of stone,
of wool and history, that solid place where I once lived;
and then there is the town which lives in me
and like the town which lived my childhood out,
it lines my veins and rings my trunk, and has a root
deep in the way I move towards tomorrow.

This other town survives
among the terraced sootfalls of my mind
where darkening time
itself grows old (as I grow old) but will not die
until my cells of thoughtful blood
forget themselves again in earth.
Were Huddersfield cut out of me
I would become a leaf in partial skeleton.

Going about the town of stone today,
I recognise it as a tune I know
played out of key, or my own voice played back on tape.
Old buildings have been scoured to new,
new buildings look as cardboard drab
as packing cases in the station yard.

So I must confess I miss
the Market Hall, that old iron reptile house
that stank of bacon, soap and sweaty socks;
and the station, black as old Victoria,
in Saint George's Square, its pigeoned columns
conducting us to hell in the classic style.

Many parts of town are little changed
or changed no more nor less than I have changed
since I last walked in them. Haunting myself
in New North Road, I know the pavement yard by yard
in my imagination, watching myself now stepping up and
down the kerbs at every minor road and drive.
I sense the temperature of my shoes, my shadow's summer density,
the active weight of stepping up and down.
Yet if I went there now to walk
with maps supplied by memory, I would soon fall.

And if along that well-known unknown road
I were to meet myself as I was then, so newly
educated, but so lightly skilled in living,
like strangers, he and I would soon discover
a life that books and talk could never span.

What I am now, but he could not yet comprehend,
is everything I learned from those I knew
and those I loved – and loving leapt from child
to fatherhood: it is the darker foliage
my sapling years began to make, and that deep root
to knowledge of myself about the world, which took to life
nourished in the stones of Huddersfield.

Cal Clothier

from GARLIC LANE

The lane runs like a thread from the town, linking
wefted row on row of houses flanking
a park, a rugby league and cricket field
that leap the river to the high-backed moors, hilled
purple heights which stand aloof and sweep
to the wind the muck that chimneys wipe
across the lane far, far below.
Mean they seem, but millstone streets belie
the life romped out in Garlic Lane.
No squalid drabness here, but line on line
of homes alight with righteousness and vice,
sin and virtue all a-tussle. Where voice
on voice flat-vowelled scrag the air
as Saturday begins to gain momentum, hour
by week-end hour; and the rugby-league crowd
jostles over white-scrubbed flag stones, carried
in a tide down Garlic Lane, past
the Misses Twitchetts' parlour which the goal-posts
peep so coyly into from the pitch.

The rugby field in summer grew buttercups like suns,
huge childhood flowers that blotted out the sins
of mills and factories; grew the valley green
a while from reaches of the meadows grown
from the farms beyond the boundaries of the town –
a textile town too quickly spawned and torn
a century before from hill and lovely dale.
The rugby and the cricket fields now dole
old meadows out along the river's course,
and buffet mills and factories and the cares
of weekday toil back into the belly of the town;
where head-scarved mams with prams turn
into shops and caffs on Saturday respite, while dad
and lad bawl lung-hard down at T'Field.

John Waddington-Feather

BARNOLDSWICK via COLNE

Here was a landscape
where no tourist coach would stop;
the picturesque was wanting
merely a mere of millstone grit
set in a rolling sea of green grey hills.
Here were mill chimneys, a family of fourteen
spaced to take advantage of what Nature had to offer
behind a sheltering hill
whose springs would water East and West
tributaring Airedale, Ribble and Canal
flowing, without prejudice either way.
The townsfolk – county named
had Yorkshire Gills and Cooks from Lancashire
hopscotched in terraces, alternate L and Y.
All weavers, kissed thread end from cops
fed shuttles into warp for cotton cloth.
The clattering looms chattered
rendering down speech to meaningless.
But women weavers gossiping, their lips
told soundless stories of the menfolk
which would prickle hairs
not only on your head.
All must have been Flat Earth Folk
the train stopped here, a single line,
outward was push and coming home was pull – so
miss the train - walk off the edge and fall
into The Unknown Land that's Lancashire.

Albert Thornton

AT RIBBLEHEAD

Whizzing stones at the beck with lazy whip
the tired hikers laze endlong down slopes,
hollowed below three peaks they have climbed –

now most are happy to loll and absorb
the sheep-brawled silence of evening sun
until the diesel brrs back to town.

Yet a few curve over the tussocks right
where a sudden breeze flicks at them left
as they swing to face the viaduct:

straight horizontal and under it, stiff;
twenty four half-circles jacked in air
by pillars no summer evening can drowse

of wind-brushed stone on invisible rock
holding unseen the steel Settle-Carlisle
that solders Whernside to far Penyghent.

The strollers look straight, then across, across,
all ways they work eyes to include this mass
before, drawn under, they stare up and through

to sense how weight is piled silent to base
(five thick, one thicker, that four times done)
where they stand on the unhewn ground between

columns the drop-headed sheep gnaw round
till they sway right back to see swung bricks float
airily tethered to sky-travelling stone.

K.E.Smith

THOUGHTS ON THE RIVER NIDD

A town, precarious on steep banks,
Its wild seams – weeds and weeping willows,
Dipping into water's greener lights –
And a river in summer, streaming.

You, rowing hard against the rhythm,
Away from a landing stage, and boats,
Bobbing gently, you pull us towards
Leafy pools, stagnant or half-obscured

By reflections of an ancient bridge;
Its arches – like Cathedral ruins –
Bode of sweet, neglected prayers,
Its windows are the moving world,

And we are passing moments, cradled
Between steep banks, our grandeur lives:
Impassioned, frail – yet intimating
How all things are held together.

Linda Marshall

PILGRIMAGES

from THE BRIDGE

We have not lost paradise; it was never found.
We are always seeking.

High over Tyne, that brown tide-swirling river,
alone I stood midway from child to man
seeing only appealing water, never
replacing always, ignoring the steel span
the arch suspending a road on which men travelled
over the sea-going ships who made this death
by their buoyant adventure a path –
but the body cavilled
till the mind found better reason, in lung salt breath
cleared for the eyes wide vision and the soul marvelled.

Living I found streams stone-impeded hastening
in triumph of foam and coruscant smooth curve
bridged by stone-trestled slabs on moors whose swerve
of hill's cut by gaunt-standing mica-glistening
cross or king's stone; by single peaceful arch
where mountain waters pound rocks to be free
in the yellowgray Galloway sea;
or, where white birch
clings to bank stones with roots that clasp and search,
by stepping stones near the islanded holly tree.

Between bends the road crosses the turbulent falls
hustling blue Morar to the lucid strait.
The driver glimpses red weed, white beach, recalls
the guidebook: 'More silver sand. Did you see the boat?
The lake is up that road to the right, dead end
far off the route. Can you hear the torrent roar?'

They pass on, they ignore
the source, life's ground –
that calm baptismal water lapping the strand,
the mysterious holy hills of the further shore.

Brian Merrikin Hill

HOLLINGWORTH LAKE

The dark deep drowning water
Reflects the harsh blue neon sign
The yellow street-lamps
And the soft moon-glow

What hungry yearning
Beneath the surface
Makes people return to gaze
At the lake they have seen before?

The shiny blackness of the water
Drowns the noise of cars
On the motorway, high above.
Causes voices to whisper
In the artificial stillness.

A cough here
Would shatter the world.

Christine England

AT PADDY END COPPER MINES (For E.G.)

Here, at Paddy End copper mine, is a density of silence
That evokes, more than the view, a sense of the altitude
A sense of the valley-lake enclosing the last emotion of
                                                    endeavour,
(Donald Campbell's grave).

Half a building, cobra of rusted cable, a post aslant,
A wheel that has detached itself from use –
Inspected, not one is more significant than the other;
The most succinct statement is underfoot,
Fragments balancing fragments, the industry's tipped waste.

The irritated vein burst from the mountain's flesh,
A shepherd in Yew-dale heard it not for thunder, but ambition
A town joined itself to;
Men drew themselves into the climate of tunnels,
Went in, knowing their body's stature a half of a standing man,
Went in, some to a deeper, sweatier marriage than farm or
                                                    lass could give.

Children may scrabble for tri-coloured rocks and hear erode
Ten static years,
Children may pass the openings of dark-eyed tunnels
Hear the darkness seep, from its trickling wet pick out a fern;
Only they scratch the memory of thunder, their curiosity
Takes a deeper breath at a thousand feet above the valley-bed.

                                                    Joan Lee

CRIPPLE SYKE

The names fascinate: 'Far Reef' and 'Bachelor'
'Poet's Corner', 'Low Fold'...
The hill where the workhouse watches
boasts of being Troy, no less,
and this hard track they call 'Cripple Syke'.

Quietly I walk the ginnels, between walls older
than the houses they border. I love this place.
It gives a sense of continuity.
Gateposts cannibalized two centuries past
stand frozen, totems imprisoned

in stone. Across a busy road a horse shelters,
its mane braided by an aching wind.
I trace a mill pond in an oiled hollow,
find a stile left without a farm.
Slabs hewn by giants bridge an ancient stream;

Drainpipes stain a darkening wall;
a weir whitens rock and weed.
Such scenes comfort me. Though red marl
and brick colour my childhood's dream,
not stone, I am at peace here.

My past and this past were made of the same iron;
the Black Country faces I recall
were drawn with the same harsh lines I see here:
the pinched look of cold, and work, and poverty.
I love this place. It is familiar to me.

Pauline Kirk

ANALYSIS OF THE SILENCE

This silence is lack of telephone-bells and traffic,
absence of feet through grass, or keels through waves,
the gagging of rumour, or radio-voice and static,

and presence of shrill wren-signals, gannet-dives –
their splash, emergence, wing-claps of self-applause
and sighs of pale, bottleglass-green sea that heaves

its sandbank mattress over: small motors of bees
that hum low over the ground: furtive crumble of walls,
and secret mitosis of cells in leaves: far cries

of squealing terns, discordant as unoiled wheels,
above the deafening roar in the hub of the world's
invisible dynamo thundering here, that feels

like silence. But here, where deft gannets pin chiffon folds
of water-scarves, I can hear, under all, the terrific
engines. Here is the axle-tree that holds

the planet in place, and controls the unsleeping traffic.

Anna Adams

FOR SALTFLEET HAVEN

Not having seen you recently, I come
At last, home.
Goodbye. I shall not
Bother you much again.
You do not notice, but
Pointless identification is my principal pain.

I have traced your story
As far as records go
Through brief mediaeval glory
To what Blake called being chartered – that *I* know.

Storms, too, have broken
Your banks and spread
Your waters over marram and samphire, taken
Away your course, denied
You identity. Well,

You're still here. I won't
Make Wordsworth's mistake with the Duddon, spell
Out prophecies that can't
Foresee dams. Yet you show
What lasts: I revert
To knowing quietness. Brief
But of all a part
(As in your swim a little leaf)
I will no more intrude
My private grief:

I am water, tide.

                                        Brian Merrikin Hill

ADLESTROP II

Yes, I remember Adlestrop – nothing there it seemed
at the dust-drab lane's fork but a large
Dutch double barn stacked with wisped
hay-bales high to the curved blue corrugate roof.

Behind, a nondescript grey
farmhouse, a gaudy enamelled tractor
its ditching-scoop poised precarious
over the pale baked earth; protruding round a corner
the sun-bleached bonnet of a battered mini.

Not a soul in sight; and no apparent possibility
of anyone ever appearing; as if time
had yielded fealty to space
and space become .
the normal sole content of everyday.

So *small* a place! One almost began to wonder
whether it had ever existed except perhaps
in Edward Thomas's heated imagination
that day in June, two wars and a world away.

We were through it before we knew
in our bright red shining hatchback;
and only a tall white-fingered wooden signpost
a half-mile on prodded us back
over the dusted road.

And there, within the wide pearl-timbered clapboard
cool of a village bus-shelter, in the shifting shades
above the slatted seat
yes, ADLESTROP! – the station sign
in dulled off-white and faded chocolate brown the unmistakeable
letters the itinerant poet must have seen
through heat-drowsed lids

'among the willows, willow-herb, and grass'
one perfect minute, while a blackbird sang.

(More than a mile away
beside a grey-tarred hump on the road to Stow
the station was demolished long ago.)

B. P. Luxton

'Black Swans', from Return to Dreamtime, 1966, Pauline Kirk.

TURN AGAIN WHITTIINGTON

Bright lights, a timeless evening
so much to see, cabs, barrow-boys calling,
the crowds and lovers walking quietly by
ignored the child.
Charing Cross or Leicester Square
or was this Piccadilly?
He didn't care, didn't matter much
this was Big City – London!
The band in uniform, inside with ale and stout
celebrating First Prize in Third Class National.
The seven-years-old with lemonade in glass
sitting outside the doorway, had no fear.
He'd been a little further South that day,
seen a vast panorama, the dramatic architecture
of the Glorious Crystal Palace
ten years before its death.
He had heard two thousand men of brass
play Elgar and Verdi with Schubert
arranged, as usual, for father's cornet solo,
and the rest, fifteen times over
and in rehearsal too.
That cursed test piece soon became a ghost,
a shadowy tune for whistling,
one which would later interfere
with concentration in examination,
or when a cat walked through an open door.

Albert Thornton

POSTCARD OF AN INDIAN CEREMONY

Dry hills and open plains,
harsh sky watching;
rock warm in the afternoon,
roads linking to Heaven.

We stand waiting our future:
the god who reveals all.
He comes by boat unseen
but known, red and gold.

Many sided, many faced,
Lord Shivah teach us.
Carry our sorrows.
Hear us; bless us.

We, the young, worship.
We wait, earth bound
among dry plains, under
drier skies – watching.

Pauline Kirk

IMAGINING AMERICA

He carried the sun in a wooden pale
and threw it out with the slops

before a breakfast of eggs over easy,
coffee, and a cigarette to bless the fire.

He offered gophers and eagle talons from his hearth
and drilled their bones into the dusty earth.

The sun rose like a tomahawk
and split the creek in two.

All day the pines bent to a blue wind,
herds grazed, he held the wolf at arm's length.

Late September the dead men came
due East from beyond the rim.

They spoke like thunder. From their wooden boats
they traded insults and poured fire down his throat.

They stretched his hide across the valley
and spun his scalp in the loom of the sky.

Bones dissolved to lemon curd
and fletched the sediments of the river bed.

Stars fell like snowdrops into the lake
and swelled the meltwater above the breaks.

In one turbulent winter
he was lost without a trace.

Andrew Boobier

ENTERING THE VALLEY OF KASHMIR: EVENING

Below, the flooded fields return
the wide clear sky, but colder yet.
Over the wash-wet ground is drawn
a fine graticulated net
in spreading Indian ink, such that
the field-banks and the knolls of land
on which the farms and poplars stand
recede across the misty plain
as distance draws the blurred mesh in.

Above, the sky is pale, and from
the pallid plain, a blur-blue range
rises till the mountains rim
the prospect with a pink-cut flange.
Now, looking back, I try to arrange
these words to make a web to hold
the images they blur – more cold
and distant now than ever, since
the words displace the experience.

Nicholas Bielby

MOROCCO: IN THE HIGH ATLAS

They might have been lovers meeting
                    by the glimmer of stars
but the stars were white candles cupped
                    in the palm of the hand.
They made a perfect picture.

They seemed to be conversing with the lights
                    as if with small, tame things.
Their language might have been birds or the river
                    chatting to the warm evening.
I couldn't distinguish a single word.

The standing figure was a man; his flame
                    seemed to project his face
into the hood of his djellabah.
                    The seated figure was
a young woman; her bowed head hovered
                    above her steady flame.

To my educated European eye the scene
                    I was watching from shadow
was Rembrandt in the High Atlas,
                    perfect chiaroscuro;
the Berbers were a small 'Nativity'.

Though I'd heard a woman in the village
                    had died in childbirth
earlier that day, and though I thought I heard
                    the young woman sob,
still I could not penetrate the art that keeps
                    two cultures apart.

Cal Clothier

FOR EVER

The sun gouged out our eyes. We stood
again outside Saint Emilion's shrine
and thanked our guide, apologised
for our half-baked French and well informed
Americans; the underground cathedral done,
already en route for another arena.

Village curator, she knew the summer trade
kept body and soul together, led us
sun-dazed through a maze of passages
to her quarters where begonias flared madly
in crazed jars. Beckoned us to peer
into an obscure corner, a shady sanctuary
for her pièce de résistance; empty
sarcophagi salvaged from crumbling
catacombs. We chilled to see how well
these sepulchral stones had served
their purpose and wished a host
of loquacious Yanks would descend
to break the ice with brash sentiments.

Pressing centimes into the crone's
creased palm we fled as if Saint Emilion's
very ghost was breathing down
our prying necks, hell bent on redeeming
our dying day with blood red wine, its source
the Gallic dust we had disturbed.

Reprieved, we drank to stupefaction.
We were in paradise. Even the sky
was star spangled and in the name
of all that is holy
would have wanted it no other way.

                                        Joyce Thornton

LIVING IN HISTORY

from PIROUETTE OF EARTH:
CHAPTER FOURTEEN: REFUGEES

Yes, everything and everyone
Was going to Madrid.
Lorries, cars, barrows, carts, horses and donkeys,
Were all being quickly loaded up.
Cats, dogs, hens, furniture, fruit, vegetables and elderly relations,
Were hastily dumped on the tops of the little carts,
Whilst others less cumbered with chattels,
Just streamed out empty handed from the village,
And joined the ragged army
On that frantic confused scramble to Madrid.

Old Pedro looked wearily on at the chaos.
The neighbours were loading up their donkey –
Quarrelling as to what should go;
Saucepans, mugs, carpets, trinkets, clothing,
All lay scattered in the dust before the house.
Bibiana was crying at having to leave her doll;
The wife was hastily wringing the chickens' necks,
So that they would have food for the journey;
While the husband angrily tied on the bundles,
And the donkey stood there patient, tired and thirsty.

Old Pedro just watched.
He did not do anything,
He just stood and looked at the turmoil.
He was seventy,
And had lived at Delitosa all his life.
Why should he move?
Surely they wouldn't trouble him –
An old man – so near to death anyway.
And so he merely stood there.

He did not feel frightened –
Just annoyed,
It was a sort of irritation,
Like receiving a visit from a tedious friend
Just as one was going to bed.

'Are you doing anything,
Or are you just standing there?'
Shouted his neighbour.
'If you're not shifting,
We'll have the loan of your donkey'.
'I'm staying here,
And my donkey's staying here also',
Declared old Pedro –
The weary wrinkles of his twilight face,
Suddenly sharpening into a noontide of defiance –
As if by making a firm stand in this small matter,
He could stem the whole tide of civil war.

The neighbour cursed,
And the wife shrugged her shoulders,
Bibiana kissed her doll,
And laid her under a bush in the garden.

'Right, that's it.
Come on, come on,
Whatever's left is left.
Come on now,
You walk the first mile –
Then daddy will give you a pick-a-back'.
They moved off –
Husband and wife and Bibiana
(The only child to survive infancy).
They had been Pedro's neighbours for twenty years,
But as the donkey staggered off
They did not even murmur 'adios'.

The old man just carried on standing there,
Leaning on his staff,
Immobilized by the weariness of it all.
All his family were dead long ago,
There was no one to come and shake him from his stupor –
To make him want life badly enough,
To tug at his sleeve
And take him away.

But by the evening it was lonely.
Only cats and a few dogs were around,
And old Pedro still just stood there,
Wishing a little that he had made the effort.
Gunfire came in a dim chorus from the south,
And as the sky darkened,
He could see the flashes
There beyond the Almonte valley –
Yes, it was getting closer – closer.

Tramp, tramp, tramp,
A gang of republican soldiers came along the track.
'Hey there grandad,
Don't just stand around
Waiting for the Moors to cut you up.
Come on,
I'll give you a pick-a-back.
There we are,
Up you go,
All right?'

There had been something about the man,
That had made old Pedro want to go with him.
'But what about the donkey?'
He suddenly said.
'Oh it will be too slow,
No – we are better like this'.

And so they tramped off through Delitosa,
The young soldier holding his strong hands,
Under the old man's withered thighs.
And as they passed by the familiar scenes,
Old Pedro looked at them with a pained strangeness –
Looked at the darkening cypresses,
Still holding themselves in prayer
To a cold unheeding God;
At the little church,
Where no doubt the pictured virgin
Stood there untroubled in the clouds of heaven;
And at the coat of arms
Above the now deserted manor house,
The bear forever holding its paws against the tree.
And as they pass,
One of the cypresses is creaking in the evening wind –
A weird strange creaking,
Like a message or a prophecy:
'Farewell, farewell,
For ever, for ever, for ever'.
Tramp, tramp, tramp,
To Madrid,
To Madrid.

Ian M. Emberson

DUTCH FARMHOUSE: CHRISTMAS 1944

i.m. Thomas Cook (1912 - 82).

Sappers are billeted here, men with crafts,
desert rats whose trails stretch back four years
through France's bocage, Italy, Palestine.
Here they have respite, brief lull in flat lands
where rough ways are planed to lowliness.
Raw days on canals, on pontoon rafts,
building bridges for following lines of troops.

The house is full. Spartan attic spaces,
soldiers' kit spread neat on boards where they sleep.
Children share their parents' room, crammed close
like snuggling sheep. Their common tongue
is that of gesture, smile and quiet respect.
Spoken words are few and broken. Late Christmas Eve
a sergeant opens up two bags, packed tight.

Spread on a bench, rich in firelight's glow,
are presents for all. Woollen gloves and stockings,
bottled beer, Hartley's jam, Capstan cigarettes.
Tomorrow a toddler will peel and taste
her first orange. Sweet and chocolate rations
are pooled and boxed, treats for little ones.
Everywhere broad beams, mirror gleams of peace.

Times to celebrate. Farm gin and advocaat,
stored in the cellar through five years of war,
are broached now. Glasses touch. No formal toasts,
only unvoiced wishes, dreams and hopes,
which are blent in children sleeping, those upstairs,
those in England and those yet to be born,
but most in the Child whose coming brought light.

The mother has made it homely,
decking with green sprigs kitchen and hallway.
A bare tree, and in a recessed corner
a simple crib, fretted from scraps of wood
by one of the soldiers, apprentice joiner.
Central figures – Mary, Joseph, ox and ass –
were here already, securely wombed in straw.

Cards on the mantelpiece, greetings from wives,
girlfriends and mothers, brothers at home,
back on leave in Bradford and Birkenhead.
The church clock chimes midnight. A gap is filled:
the infant is lodged in his crib. Time for bed.
The farmer must visit his cow-shed
to check on a new-born calf, premature, struggling.

The sergeant goes out with him, to carry
an extra torch. Flatnesses stretch away
through Europe's darkness to far distant camps:
there prisoners freeze in huts as arc lights glare.
Here the well-primed oil lamp sways gently,
casting shifting circular beams. A wild swing
from a north-east gust, but the flame burns on.

John Cook

WORKING ON THE CASTLEFIELD CANAL 1820

I was young once – now old at twenty-four.
Each unlit dawn I walk five miles to work
to lay rough-hewn blocks along their canal.
Luck leaps in rich pockets, leaves us deafened, dumb.
but the pathways we build give me tired satisfaction

It all started here, in our blood and guts.

Not paid till weeks' end, no cold tea in my bottle.
God, so little for the children, what can they scrounge?
We'll chew dandelion leaves and try to toast swedes.
This labour separates my meat from my bones,
its grime slimes our mouths, hands, clothes
the slime we dig out for their freshwater canals.

It all started here, in Castlefield's blood and guts.

Foreman strides up, warm coat, early as usual
 'We'll finish the towpath this month, if it kills me'
May not kill you, but a mate's sure to drop dead.
Spades on our shoulders, we march to their carts
we dig hours all morning, we dig with bruised shoulders.
I warm to the quartz streaks in the old stone
crowned by those weird, proud turrets on the bridge:
weeks of hoisting brick on brick over rough ropes.

It all started here, in our blood and guts.

Some days we sing, till our throats stop croaking
then soundlessly screaming, we're working cadavers.
After 600 wounded, too scared to revolt.
Too often storms brew in this muddied, damp air
rain, rain, forty days, rain, rain, forty nights.
Our steps lead to nowhere, start to crumble,
girders drown, locks sink, our names drown.
This work, their dream, brings us accidents, death
we build while they dance, we dig vast tombstones.

It all started down here, from our blood and guts.

Olga Kenyon

Cityscape, vignette from *Pennine 25*, 1991, Albert Thornton.

A VISION OF CABEZA DE VACA (Lost in Mexico from 1528 to 1536)

The moon cuts shadow under our ribs
as we come on a village, adobe houses
appear an oasis etched on moonlight,
gleam like the armour we lost when we lost
all but our bodies, the means to suffer.

Blanched to a skin manned by bones,
we have blood and our breathing
to prove we are men, and the hungry light
jerking our eyes. We are down to mercy,
gratitude, love, down to humanity.

Poorer than us, the villagers come
feeling our bones, touching our pain,
to bring us food; they are mothlight phantoms
coming and going, crooning, comforting,
bearing the moon with their gifts.

No longer conquistadors, simply men
forked naked into the breathless
Inferno of nature, this new world:
is this vision of love the ghostly hush
of vampire lunacy sipping our brains?

Are we spellbound from humping the sun's gold
too far that we dream these angels of Jacob
coming and going in threads of motion,
a web of moonlight? Heaven is silver,
God the spider spinning us into His love.

Cal Clothier

CROICK CHURCHYARD

The deadend of two roads,
north or south of the Carron –
the moors from Croick stretch
barren now into Strathoykell

'Glencalvie people was in the churchyard
here, May 24, 1845'

This message, their names, in English,
scratched for ever on the diamond panes,
cries across the years
The fingers that wrote
point at us

They saw their own language dying
as surely as they saw their homes destroyed
It would not be Gaelic sheep
grazing their old pastures denaturing the soil

This one memorial remains
long after the stones
of their homes have merged
irrevocably into the heather
where not even the grouse
are safe past autumn

Gerald England

THE BADGER STONE

– Rombalds Moor, Yorkshire

A stone badger, crouched
on the wet moor
– haunch and snout –

Intricate cupped rings
fill flank and side.
Bronze-age doodlings

are they? Shadows pass
over cold stone,
over bent grass.

Did willow, birch and pine
shield once this place
and hide a shrine?

Meanings, guesses twinned
with blood and stone
tease the wind.

Seed where no soil is
may germinate
and grow like this

shape of ancient pain;
double-edged sun?
...the cupped rain.

Mabel Ferrett

THE FLAX BLEACHER'S DAUGHTER

They found the flax bleacher's daughter
drowned in the mill dam,
naked, cold as swamp,
haltered by the wet swaddle of her hair,
eyes open, blacker than bird cherries.

They carried her to the chapel,
properly shawled and veiled,
the drench of hair coiled and wrapped,
pennies blanking the pools of her gaze,
to be laid out in the small light of beeswax candles
which opened the dark in constellations.

She couldn't rest
but lay waiting under turf and heather,
creeled by sycamore roots,
hollowed and caved by the consuming seasons
to socket and bone,
lured from her anchored skeleton,
a soft glimmer at the lip of the dam,
a curve of light breaking the surface,
a stream of silver spilling over oily water.

The chapel,
now little more than a garner of stone,
crumbles inwards, eroding under a pall of bindweed,
its rafters, once the roost of souls,
unrigged by gales and colonised by rooks.
The flax bleacher's daughter whispers,
stirring the night air, rousing bat and barn owl,
pursues her secret into a niche of light.

Lesley Quayle

PORTRAIT OF A FOREMOTHER

You watch warily from an old snapshot,
leaping to life over forty-five years
and wearing the old black apron –
large pocketed for holding sweets
or string for making cats-cradle.
Your purple headscarf, white-spotted,
knotted behind to make a dust cap.
I recall the colour of your dress too –
blue and white, leaf-patterned,
run up from a remnant at four-three a yard,
bought from a stall in the Harrow Road.

Why do your colours dazzle
when the snap is monochrome
while the child standing beside you
wears colours I've forgotten?
We stand to attention in your backyard
fixed forever between coal-hole and fence post,
watching the birdie in Mum's box-brownie.

You told me of an East End childhood
when weary Jews walked from the Docks
bearing bundles and exotic speech.
You linked me to Greatgrandad
who fled Prussian militarism,
married an English country girl
and was stoned by a mob in 1915 –
in spite of three sons in the trenches.
You reared your younger brothers
after Greatgrandma died in childbed
and fretted for them later
as they fought in France or in the Dardanelles.

Somewhere there was a husband
who sought consolation in a beer glass
until you threw him out for good.

It was you who taught me to read,
your hand moving over the page
as I related words to pictures.
You got me my first library ticket
and took me to Garbo films
which I thought soppy.
I listened in the bomb shelter
as you counted the bombs down
and fulminated against Hitler.
I failed to understand the meaning
but I understood courage –
it was you who taught me to endure.

I return the snap to the drawer,
that wary look is too much like
the reflection in my mirror.

Jean Barker

NAILHOUSE

My people made nails like these,
beaten sharp, cut from the rod.
These shears and bellows
are the sort they once used.
The museum grate is filled with paper
but some sense of toil touches us:
the tiny window, the rotten door.

In a nailhouse like this, six by four,
greatgrandmama kept her children fed.
being widowed she had little choice,
and her mother, widowed too and aged,
had less. So they sweated together
and sang their hymns. In Summer
they would have stripped to the waist.
The children worked too; their play
was sweeping and packing; blowing bellows.

The cottages are desirable today;
plant pots sit on nailhouse windows.
The young favour homes with character
so long as they have baths and videos.
History is marketable now.
For Greatgrandmama, History was sweat
and a widow's bag of nails.

Pauline Kirk

BOMBED

Leipzig
ancient city of my loves

You I can't know
without pictures and re-buildings

flakked out
city streets where thoughts could ease
ease open pavements

Can a word
cover

the cry
of a dying child?

Anna Taylor

HEADHUNTERS

1

You ventured from the forest.
On my television screen I watched you coming
with a silence no less grave than his
upon a peak in Darien.

You were brown bright, the cocoa fruit of
darkness naked with the leaves, you were
chattering in the seeded grass like parakeets:
laughing animal colours you were yet men.

Your centuries of isolation had been
edited away. The credits rolled, you came on cue
offering spears and primitive tools
for axes, cooking pots, plastic dolls
as white as your teeth, vaccination and
empty bottles - you fluted across their mouths
as freely as children would: you
entered Mankind almost
surreptitiously.

And all the while our camera was measuring
every gesture of hand and eye,
customs, breasts, delight and shyness – all
absorbed into the chemical darkness of our film.

We have taken your spirit.
We shall destroy you, ovum and sperm,
file you away in the footnotes of time;

evolution has left you no means of protection
now against men who evolve at their will.
You have laughed in our living room,
fragile creatures,
and for that honour you will now pay
as Atahualpa and Montezuma
paid with the blood of the very sun.

2

I knew you only, as a boy,
from adventure stories: in dugout canoes
you shadowed in the swamps of the anaconda Amazon,
shrieking blood and magic as you gutted missionaries,
and you shrank explorers' heads to the grimace of a nut.

Is it that same fear of a dreaming child
makes men rape you, burn you, castrate you;
are you chimeras to be exorcised from
the terror we bring in our shrunken minds;
or is it the nervous, omnivorous forest
wills us to shoot what looks like man?

Surely it's more than superstition,
more than demonology, watches,
waits while you finish a pot or basket
and stamps the museum code into your culture?

Surely more than our eyes have turned
to plastic when we cannot see
your bark-brown body felled with a tree,
when we cannot hear in your picturesque swansong
(long since our own song)
the voice of the woodworm auctioneer?

But one does not need any knowledge of trade
entirely to vanish

in the small change of Progress. And you have been sold.
The Deed by which your hunting ground
has been acquired describes the land as 'clean' –
unoccupied except by animals. Technology and capital
through whom all sins are now absolved
requires your blood to lubricate its veins.

It needs no concept on your part
of property, whose culture goes
with herds that die and fruit that drops unripe:
you have become, who never were,
a free-fire zone in the progress war.

3

Your noon has passed, Ephemera:
have you not savoured blood in the rain,
blood in the veins of the newest leaf, the monkey cry?

You will be murdered, but genocide's only
killing a people, and here you barely
qualify in your evergreen nakedness.

Should you survive, you will be taken to lie at the base
of our civilisation; fatherless, heirless,
you will know ignorance,
you will acquire poverty of the latest model.
The dogs of the slum will not beg from you.

Our men will come and record your myths (from
tribe to archive in one generation),
seeking to find in your culture proof
that our greed and cruelty have their source
in the primitive mind,
and not in his mind who can fell a forest
as painlessly as if trees were men.

Take what comfort you can from this
as we watch you die,
you are not getting special treatment while
everywhere we enslave and exploit. Our heads no longer
relate to man.

We are eagles betrayed by our wings,
we are fish that drown as they breathe,
we are antelopes run to death by our legs,
we are jaws that devour the mouth.

Pity us, Cannibals,
Headhunters,
pity us, for we have coined the world
only to purchase the world.

Cal Clothier

A LAST NOTE, 1917

Stumps of trees
blackened through the stumps
limbs

Brains spewing down your shoulder
crunched still to a rifle butt

Blessed with the canons
and the 'spirit of the bayonet'
you said you'd abandon.

For a couple of months
your chest caved
rats, also charred
when your pals managed
to recover you.

And the hugs and the kisses
I wrote as a last but, but
not, as I thought, farewell

A greeting for your 18th birthday;
your first abroad. Such excitement lifted you
into that London train,
already fading

They found my xxxxes fluttering –
some blasted pocket, they said.

The top left one I gave
a stitch to on that –
our last evening at home?

Meandering
benighted
the afternoon

Is this what remains

That woman your sisters
still call
mother?

Anna Taylor

THE SOUND OF HARRIS

What is this sound upon the air, a faint
susurration of the marram-grass fronds?
Rather a coronach that fills with dread,
drawn as it were from the landscape's heart,
a long low keening with the measured tread
of generations of the island dead.

Or that year's final crop of families
straggling the strand with their belongings
(creels, spades and bibles) freeing from the throat
the communal wail of the dispossessed,
which, as the cortege enters in the boat,
fails to a single bag-pipe's reedy note.

Drowned now beneath the waves' absolving sound
'husinish husinish' upon the sand.

John Killick

OLD JEWISH CEMETERY WITHIN THE VIENNESE NECROPOLIS

Along the bleak and windswept lanes
of old Vienna's field of bones
the front doors of the dead make clear
in gilded letters: the remains
of the remembered dead lie here.
    In multitudes, entombed in peace,
    good families increase.

And to this vast necropolis
at Halloween, old children come
to say their prayers, kindle flames
and trim encroaching wilderness
from their good Christian names
    which the obliterating shroud
    of nature seeks to hide.

Beyond the edge of Christendom
the Israelitish graves begin,
and they are pierced and prison barred
by sapling trees, entangled in
barbed briars, brambles, old-man's-beard;
    for here lie ancestors of smoke –
    the childless folk.

The grandfathers of ash arise
as thickets where the foxes lurk;
their monuments are in disguise,
anonymous with ivy, wound
around them, and caged angels speak:
    A glittering river has been drowned
    in barren ground.

Now ivy, ash and old-man's-beard
repeat the shocking message, heard
in silence till a hidden wren
and blackbird amplify it. Nature's note
bears witness, has become the thighbone flute
    that whistles Murder at the carnival,
    accusing all.

                                    Anna Adams

CHESSMEN OF WALRUS IVORY

– Part of a hoard of 178 found at Vig,
Lewis, about A.D. 1200.

Falling in ranks
at wave
of careless hand
mustered again
count eight and eight
all present
nameless
sexless
expendable sacrifice.

It is no coincidence I think
that the pawns
are gravestones
faceless
uniform
wearing their livery
of Celtic convolution.

THAT PIECE IS FLAWED
TAKE IT.
Knight leaps across the board, obedient.
How strange.
I had observed that knight sometime
and thought a softness lit
the eye he cast upon her
yesterday.

Poor pawn
he'll find
and take
another.

Better though
that she cry not
'Why?'
chance not identity.

Can you speak little faceless one
and cry out
'Why?'
challenge ascribed non-entity.

Mabel McGowan

EXTRAVAGANZA

Tucked in a terrace of small
  houses
it functions to help the aged
with forties bric-a-brac
tired suits, yellowing lampshades
and tacky browning paperbacks.
I feel weighed down with old.

Look up. Hanging from dark
  rafters –
exotic underwear, revealing,
  erotic.
The briefest of briefs rub gus-
  sets
with calf-length frilly drawers;
boned red basques, black laced,
touch up flouncy petticoats.

I am spirited to Montmartre,
to the world of Toulouse
  Lautrec,
to paint charity-shop ladies
who kick high, draw wide cir-
  cles
with toes of lace-up boots.
They flash frou-frou skirts,
display frilled bottoms for
  posterity.

I draw the shop's till guardian,
slim his beer belly
into black drainpipe trousers.
He dons a battered opera hat,
dances for an evening's absinthe.
I paint to the music of the
  Moulin Rouge
a nineteenth-century raffish
  glamour.

But friends lead me outside
talking of jam and the WI
  Market.
I walk through a world of
  discarded clothes,
disintegrating Archer novels
– and charity for the old –
to a new, empty Millennium-
  domed Britain.

Jean Barker

**Cover design for *Brakken City*, 1997,
Linda Marshall.**

OVID IN EXILE

– The poet reflects to a visitor on the death
of the emperor Augustus, who had banished
him to the outer reaches of the Roman Empire.

All visitors from Rome are VIPs –
through here to feel the wood-fire flush your cheeks
and find how like the natives I've become
though there's a hypocaust installed as well
to prevent yet hairier transformation.
Still – as you *might* have noted – Rome this isn't
but Tomis at Dacia's edge where tribes
raid into town with snow each winter
and poets lapse from Latin into Getic
(they were *very* pleased with me, Apollo).

But to your matter: just before he died
in stifling summer Rome you saw him,
courteous and cool as ever? Of course
we knew within a few weeks even here:
'Long live Tiberius'...' For the Senate
and the People'... in short, cheers, games and booze.
And so he's beaten me to the Shades as well
to trash my reputation with the great...
What? Thought of a return to Rome's ruled out –
I sense Tiberius would forebear to cheer,
endorse that signature of banishment.

The first indictment at least was made clear,
my *Art of Love* charged with corrupting youth,
encouraging boys and girls to ogle,
solitary soldiers to spill their seed
(collapse of stout empire all Ovid's fault –
as if it needed downhill help from me).

But the second charge was different,
not fit to be brought before the public
because too shaming an emperor's name:
in short, bard Ovid when graciously asked
to submit all work for imperial *fiat*
made metric response: 'By Jupiter, no! –
subdue my shape-changing magic words
to the carved parrot-speak of imperial law?'

Your hidden thoughts I infer from your face –
just poet's luck to avoid a chariot,
a thoughtful gift of dagger or hemlock –
but cunning Augustus grew yet kinder
mellowing when all knew he *could* kill
as with his all-controlling blandness
he steered me to irrelevant exile...
Here? By the Black Sea life's been deadly kind
since the citizens met me at the gate:
'Great honour...Tomis...Welcome, great Ovid...'
One local big-wig encouraged his daughter
who, bored and twenty, gave good greeting
until next morning she combed her hair to speak:
'You were one of my grandad's favourites
and great-aunt Tertia asked me to ask you
if you identify with Pygmalion?'
In that one moment I transformed from man
to this bird-stained, greybeard statue you see –
my ultimate metamorphosis here.
So it's wine, few women and work for me
as I guard this no-man's land of freedom
between empire's edict and howl of wolves
(too little time left for me to fear either).

I was no overt critic of tyrants
to charge with freedom's banner unfurled,
no Cato's virtue attended a life
not quite so naughty as I'd have hoped.
But I *was* one who spellbound lead to gold,
who managed to prise that imperial hand
up from its clamping vice-grip on vision.
Free to inscribe in your citizen brain
fables of life's *Metamorphoses*
I magically conjured a stage of dreams,
menageries of Gods, of beasts and men
whose braying chorus chants 'nothing holds firm
and everything will become what it's not',
where censors and soldiers embrace and dance
with fauns and centaurs whizzed from wings and flies
and poetry's flux seeps back from your sleep
till you rise to banish this empire of spectres...
first Ovid's auditor merits a drink.

K.E. Smith

A WORLD OF NEIGHBOURS

ORKNEY BUS

Mr Ward of Derby looking through the window
of the Stromness-Kirkwall bus at his tenth glimpse
of the Stones of Stenness, the Ring of Brogar
and the light over heath and water, told me
about them and his longer explorations
which made this annual brief sight ecstatic.

The first Summer he had come with his dear wife,
the second alone. He would come every year
though now he merely walked about in Kirkwall –
even that was enough to fill all fifty
weeks spent in his little garden in Derby,
those few square yards behind a terraced cottage.

God, when, looking at great men and states, you think
to burn the world, pray to Mr Ward of Derby.

                                    Brian Merrikin Hill

DEATH OF A NEIGHBOUR

I was never a friend of hers, but yet the street
  is diminished by her dying
for me, at any rate. We have lived
here seven years now, trying
to fit in; to know and be known. When we came
  she welcomed us with a wave
  of the hand and a smile, as who should say,
  'Pleasant to see again
windows lit up across the road
  through the threatening rain,
  plants in the rockery
and children bickering on the top step,
  giving vitality
to the old husk, the shell of the old house.'

I was not a friend of hers; yet, as a mouse
  secretly enters, seeking
a home inside your home, moulding its life
upon the pattern of your making,
advance, retreat, as you go out and in
    – conversely – so did she
  enter the habitual pathways of our living,
  quietly, in little things –
  accustomed generosities, offer
  of tools for gardening, exchange of gifts, and chat
at birthdays and at Christmas; and because
  each drew her curtains at
the usual hour, the cheerful, daily wave.

Two weeks ago, in the unexpected warmth
  of a spring day, the sun shining,
crocuses bright in the rockery, yellow
and purple and white combining,
a cortège passed and, according to custom, to honour
  the dead, at each house curtains were drawn,
    and women moved silent and grave at their usual jobs,
    unprying, behind it all;

yet glad, when that was done that courtesy asks,
  to pull back the curtains and call
  out to each other...so
she, jauntily, waved across to say
  'It wasn't our funeral! No!
We're still alive. The sun shines for our pleasure.'

The sun still shines. The warm spring days grow stronger
  and the rowan at my gate
buds greenly for the summer. I must plant
primulas soon, and isolate
the small buds of anemone and thrift
  from the robust London Pride
  and purple periwinkle. She
  would walk with slow movement
to savour individually
  the colour, scent
  and poise of every plant the garden grew,
glad in the coming of the spring again
  with promise of a new
miraculous flowering after the winter's cold.

No! We were never friends; too far apart
  in taste and activity
to touch each other. Yet, is it that we stood
closer than friends can be?
In one short fortnight everything's confusion;
  the waving hand, the smile
  withdrawn for ever from my casual glance
  when the time's late.
Now she is gone where all is ignorance.
  The black hearse waits.
  It is her funeral.
The sun evokes the yellow crocuses,
  birds sing; but that is all.
Today I pull my curtains back alone.

                                        Mabel Ferrett

Figures, from ***Webbed Skylights of Tall Oaks*,**
Pennine Poets Anthology, 2002, Nicholas Bielby.

THE MODEL LODGING HOUSE

The marks upon the wall in fading blue
made patriotic white against red brick.
Each letter peeling, then
falling like broken eggshell.
Only men entered, lean-boned, clean-shaven
pale but proud
all thinly clothed in reach-me-downs
from pawnbroker or jumble sale.
Some were soft-spoken Pals from Accrington
flat capped, clog ironed, tallow-candled men
in this Accrington red brick house
lid off at seven, into the shed and back at half-past five.
Tramp weavers, theirs a bunch of skills
which easily accommodated varieties of shuttle
warp and weft, and speed of picking sticks
on four-shaft dobbies, or
high-fashion coloured silk-top beams.
A ration of four looms each.
Came the normality of six apiece
robotic, automatics finding picks,
tramp weavers disappeared,
those knowing Mons, Amiens and the Somme
vanished to God knows where.
No longer well scrubbed floor,
carbolic wooden bench and table
tin mug and chipped enamel plate,
these men, could they be weaving
uniforms for another breed of soldiers
fitting out both sides in Ethiopia or Spain?

                                        Albert Thornton

THE SHOPKEEPER

Again I nod towards him as I pass the shop
he casts away from, feeding the grey-black
Bradford pigeons (stalked out of public space
now guano is adjudged a hazard)
on his patch of grass with unsold slices
and wonder if importance – being at work –
and columned emails can embrace more truth
than lounging for more words about whatever.

Our conversations have grown longer –
as he skims hexagonals from the till
and hovers them towards me, I reach out
my hand above the counter-wall between us.
Then he speaks out urgently and quickly so
Punjabi accent and my dulled ears join,
reduce our contact to a nodding head.
Yet we prize our topics – weather
with its honed Yorkshire exactitude
of grumbling; student targets
with transient hopes that he might lever back
the falling takings of his shortening hours.

He cuts the semi-skimmed, the non-meat pasties,
and odd shelves re-emerge from tins
to ache long whiteness through the afternoons –
(the Late Store round the corner's Radio 1,
the impersonal choice and fullness that we crave)
I know nothing of his history though
his crimped white hair and upright stance
evoke the dusty drill-grounds of the Fifties,
pukkah pride of Pakistan regiments,
the once young men all independent backbone.

Now and forever he must live alone,
which makes me all the more envision
that man of destiny some thirty years ago
kicking up leaf-drift under sodium lamps,
smelling the Bradford fog and knowing
he is one who has chosen life
in a Northern Frontier land.

One week next year or the year after that
he will turn away the perishable van,
unplug the freezer, leave the shelves to rise
until the Transit man takes tins and packets,
leaving him thin wads of cash in hand
to close a shop that no-one else would buy
and then...the second great decision to be made –
one-way to dusty scrub beyond a bungalow
casting bread to grey-white Punjab pigeons,
respected as one who has travelled far
to return with snowy hair and sudden speech?
Or logging students with the sweeping rains,
waiting to feed the grey-black Bradford pigeons,
seen as eccentric by children on the street
though harbouring unregarded wisdom?

Homewards I pass empty grass, meshed windows,
signs that the sage plans further journeys
though outbound or inbound I have no wit to say.

K.E. Smith

GIVE US THIS DAY

She always answered first knock,
did her wash before her shift
leaving the dolly tub to sweeten in the sun
by her back steps, and sheets to bleach
across the backstreet on a shared line.

She made the dough for the daily bread
before she scurried to the weaving shed
already at her loom by the second siren
her generous form leaning over the beam
sensitive fingers smoothing slubs.

The tackler keen and ready to give a hand
for reaching in, while thundering beams
silenced speech – eyes meeting
through the heddles, keeping tryst,
patterns emerging on the cloth,

cut out, like life on cards
dropping and rising rhythmically.
Then when knots were tied
she reached inside her pinafore
for a soft, warm breadcake
for the tackler's pains
to keep the thread continuous.

Joyce Thornton

IN THE CHILDREN'S WARD

She wears a saffron sari below a zig-zagged
blue cardigan, thin elbows angled like a bird's wings,
she fumbles the hasp of the crib,
jogs the cord that hooks her son
to a colourless sack of saline.

And all night she guards him,
rigid in an upright chair,
clasping the ribs of the cot.
Her face below its shawl
is an inverted tear.

Sharing the same sterile geography,
equally remote, we smile
when our eyes catch, each of us close
to the pulse of the drip –
the clear liquid bleeding into the vein.

Judith Bolland

LONG-STAY CASE

This was his universe except for meals and yard
Garden and workshop, this four-walled place;
He had a bed in it, a cupboard full of
Drawers but nothing else to fill the space
Where others would have pictures, shelves,
The hundred things that grace a room
And make it home; he had no need of them
He said, they were encumbrances to reason;
We thought him cracked, a creaking loom
Quite off the rails, and his remonstrances
Were lost on us; but it was he was free,
We bound, he sober, we hedged in with circumstance;
We left him on his pillar with his thoughts
Delighting in its desert emptiness, a bird
Not wanting baubles who possessed the world.

S.L. Henderson Smith

PICTURE POSTCARDS

After she died, he began collecting
picture postcards, bought
at auctions, bound and boxed.
He liked these glimpses
of a brighter world
Hutton-le-hole from the moors,
the promenade from Galley Hill.

He liked the greetings,
Benedictions, variations
(*weather here, wish you were lovely*).
He liked to hear what people like:
*Bexhill pleasant, Hastings
rather loud for us.
Not doing bad at whist.*

He liked the sense of family
(*the girls are pony trekking*);
and ritual (*fish and chips
in Whitby*). Auntie Jeanie
writes that *Rye's a charming place.*
Uncle Joe's PS.
Back for Sunday's match.

Most of all he liked the jokes,
however lame. Of picturesque
thatched cottages – *hovels.*
*Tell the lads in Planning:
Knock 'em down!* Or this
from Sandringham: *popped in on E
and P, who send their kind regards.*

Ed Reiss

DIGGING

The labour of his breath
shaped cowlicks in the frosted air
as, hunched into familiar tweed,
sweat and tobacco cured,
he rested by the old barrow.

The toil, across level ground,
the heft of limbs,
resisting drag and ache
of palsied lungs,
exhausted him.
A small, chill wind intruded,
thickening the cramped space in his chest.

God, how he used to dig,
slicing and turning the black earth,
the pure exhilaration of work
palpable in rhythms of muscle and bone.
Crumbling the clay divots by hand,
he harried the root boles
of nettle, sorrel, ground elder,
shaking them free,
tossing them to the old barrow,
till he had fleshed the dark soil
from its wild skin.

Now he stands on the thin crust of snow
in his old man's solitude,
withdrawing his presence,
fording his memories.

Lesley Quayle

NO ONE FORGETS

Miss Phillipson, Miss Phillipson, why
did you smell and look so musty?
Did you sleep in a cupboard and wash in a pond
each day before you taught us?
No Dickens or Brontë could have dredged you up,
no crack designer have concocted
your brown crimplene suits
and yes it's a cliché but your tights did scratch
as you marched between the desks, barking
as we heard it 'where the bee sucks there suck I'

and yes, Miss Phillipson, you did
suck, we all thought, especially
the girls who learned from you they had
the wrong names or faces.

For my sins I let you sign my hymn book,
acknowledging the fact
that you were getting out before us
off down south, of course –
but what was your parting shot? –
Your exhortation for a girl to
make the most of what she'd got?
(Later I threw the book and
your *bons mots* into the Rochdale Canal):
'be good sweet maid
and let who will be clever'?

Thanks pal. Good teaching.
Right on sister.
Thanks, Miss Phillipson.

Julia Deakin

THE MOWER

I.

Before each dawn he placed his face –
not the face of success, but a survivor's face –
to a hole rubbed in the steam on the glass

whilst his oil-lamp fed on a bedroom stink
of mail-order cosmetics, of pullets and cows,
some traded long since and now become ghosts
in the fibres of trousers or an itchy blouse.

II.

Work! He'd promised her nothing else!
That excused him, in both their minds:
he didn't read Sartre, grow and break faith
like you and I.

       He walked out in the flux
of unendurably cold and cyclic light
that stretched and fell like milk upon the valleys

hearing the hiss of rain on his hay
or a wind, as it blew his sheds away.

III.

In the moonlight before dawn he scythed
a track for the machine to ride.
He was always the first to start!
Not because he was less weather-wise
about the way the leaves blew,
or crows flew:
he was just too impatient
to learn from being rained-out.

Under his hat, the sweat
messed like a fowl's nesting box
as he cut and cut and cut the flames
of earth, and with an erotic sway
laid a silver street
of blundering insects whilst the red air came
and the vast smell stirred me in our sheets.

Was someone laughing at him? What
I saw of him was a tilt of black hat
that signalled 'I don't need to please
anyone' floating on grass
that hissed away from the breeze.

Glyn Hughes

IN MEMORY OF WILLIAM COLEMAN, AGED TWO
(for Margaret and Colin)

An autumn-out-of-season, white and pink,
the clotted cherry blossom shreds and sifts
its random petals down the air. They sink
and, brushed by eddies, settle into drifts.
William is dead, who once held both hands out
to grasp life like a gift or flower. If will
and love had been enough, there is no doubt
that you, who gave him life, would hold him still.

There is no comfort, only holding grief
steadily in empty hands, until
time imperceptibly brings some relief,
when, guilt and anger fading, what you feel
of grief and loss becomes a gift: as if
the holding had itself become a pearl.

Nicholas Bielby

GREEN AS A TOMATO, GREEN AS A BANANA

Out of the door of impossibility
comes Katie Milligan
from the Kwakiutl Territorial Fisheries Commission
with her red sea urchin survey.

Out of the door of impossibility
ambles Mbaba Mwana Waresa
in a torn zebra skin.
Lightning zoops across the sky!

Out of the door of impossibility
in the middle of the galaxy
billow stars, pulled by a black hole
two million times heavier than the sun.

Good luck to them! Good luck, Mbaba!
Katie, I've not forgotten you.

                                        Ed Reiss

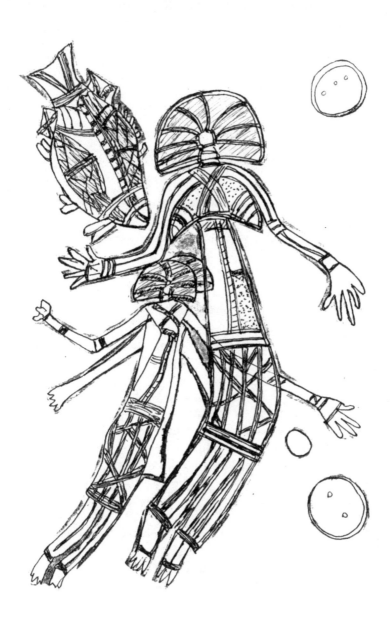

Dreamtime Figure, from *Return to Dreamtime*, 1996, Pauline Kirk.

A STILLNESS OF THE SPIRIT

CAERHÛN CHURCH

A stillness of the spirit lies
inside these walls
like the strange lull that centres in a storm.
The chill of ancient worship wraps me round
as sunlight falls
across the silence, radiant but cold,
to fire the dust of sanctity with gold.

No flame of passion lights the candles now
yet to this place
men must have brought their agonies and griefs
come running here with bursting gratitude
for favours granted or a hidden grace,
to praise the God whom their great faith made real.

No doubt that silver fox Hypocrisy
has stalked this aisle
feasting upon the flesh of ignorance
with cruel teeth but sanctimonious smile.
But now no trace of bitterness remains
to spoil the light of this serenity
and here Man's inky passions leave no stain:
the brush of time has white-washed long ago
the sins that one time seemed indelible.

Where is the peace which passes understanding?
Is this cool calm
a freezing balm of partial anaesthesia
for bruised souls?
and is the quiet with which this air
is filled, the essence of much praying
now distilled?

Oh are you there, the God to whom they cried,
holding inside Yourself their fright and mine
waiting to cauterize with flames of love
the hate by which You are still
crucified?

                                    Mary Sheepshanks

HYMNS ANCIENT AND MODERN

To what can we sing out our celebration
if God is absent? Oneness dissolves.
Small cells or large cells, such separation!
Outside or inside, nothing resolves.

A crowded mirror, a star-speck, a bird:
how can we find one maker, one made?
And yet our praises sing themselves, unanswered,
almost believing the harmonies they've played.

                                    Trevor Innes

AMBER GAMBLER

I can't stop now
the whips are at my back
I can't stop now
the time's not there to rest and look
The dog is barking, the baby cries,
the postman is knocking at the door
I can't stop now
the milk is boiling over
Though butter clogs in my arteries
I'll keep on trying
to answer the phone
go seeking more
from those who want themselves to stop
If I don't stop soon
I'll spin through the hole
at the bottom of the whirlpool
or crash over the cliff
The wolves are chasing me
I can't stop now
Will I need a pension
or just a box?
How can I dream
if I never sleep?
The lights are on
perpetual amber
I am gonna stop
but not now

Gerald England

WAITING

If I could walk on water
I should turn left on the canal
at the sign to Sowerby.
I'd have only the short way then
through the valley, before the last steps
up to your small green sanctuary.

There, surrounded by foxgloves,
you stand sentinel upon your life,
sharing their gift of spreading out delight,
digging deep to laughter in your most Irish way.
Gaelic must have words for beauty that is yours.

When I saw you lately, with your proud head
tilted in that way, I wished that I could sculpt
or draw the grace of your complexities.
Meanwhile I see you in your lush space,
tall and intricately stamened
the markings of your hopes and fears
etched, like the foxglove's patterning
on strong and supple stem, marbled velvet
green-chaliced purple, white, the liturgies of your life
upright and bending, unbreaking in the breeze,
a rooted, self-seeded, gracious harvest. Waiting.

Josie Walsh

NOTRE DAME DE HÉAS

I watched nine herons fly from Kinlochmoidart:
I am not there to know if they return.

Earth centred peace by sea-washed grass among mountains:
An oil platform now creates a different place.

I have heard songs in the company of girls
Sitting folded in the knees of fathers
With eyes imagining an ancient fiction
That unified mind and body in achieved grace:
Their children now have themes foreign to me.

Three hooded men did not greet me on the road to Hexham:
My car broke down near Coventina's well.
Walking among apple trees I heard no poem from Elijah
When late frost nipped the blossom.

Sages in their walled gardens tell their fame to the tulips:
My garden is rented, windswept, grows nettles, goosegrass.

I loved the marsh montbretia by a house called *Arra Venten*:
Others bought the place; I merely passed by

As now, briefly in your dark shrine, Lady of Snows,
On the way from Sauveterre to Perpignan
(Or Newcastle on Tyne to life's other city)
Travelling deviously, finding stone or flower in off-beat valleys,
I stop to admire your habit of surviving avalanches
To make here for the faithful a destination none of my
                                        journeys reach.

Help me, for them Mother of God, Queen of where they are
                                        and are going:
I return among people keen to annotate the bee trapped by the
                                        window
Not join its persistent search for air, flower, hive.

Grant me your triumph over ice falling among jagged rocks.
Be where I arrive when I've found the way.
Teach me to know why, lady of the bright snow,
You find this darkness holy.

Brian Merrikin Hill

CHRISTMAS EVE

Is there any difference between birth and death?
The breaking of the womb when life with trembling starts
And the tomb's slaking when with steps of stealth
Spirit forsakes time's old familiar loom and parts?

The one is coming, the other going
Beginning one and end the other;
But who can say we have not been before
And birth which seems from nothing sprung
Is rather corridor-opening of a door;
We have forgotten what that side was sung
And none can this side ask another.

They said that Christ was born, and drank their ale,
But I knew Christ was dead, the gospel stale,
All hope forlorn, until I kindling thought
His birth and death were one, the difference nought,
For as I at His manger laid my head
I was by nail-pierced hand with wafers fed.

S.L. Henderson Smith

WOOD CARVING, XV CENTURY

This 500-year-old carving of the Christ
before his crucifixion, scourged and whipped,
the blood-marks on his shoulders, facing now
the terrible reality of pain

                        gazes through unfocussed eyes
at her he loves.
                    Human, he touches me more nearly, so,
than in his Godhead!

                    Unknown carver,
whose name I would breathe in prayer, you teach
that those who love tap the creative springs
and life begets life, not only through the flesh.
Through wood and word something strange is passed.

                                All life
is vulnerability, the flayed creature, bare,
plaything of social man and, to my shame,
sometimes of me, too! Yet still the tree,
the Cross's cousin, feels the prick of nails,
and how they pierced her giving hands also,
and how he knew they would. Words blur
in the market-place and lose the edge of truth.

                    This wood endures.

                                Mabel Ferrett

WIND

This is the wind
  that catapulted clouds
    over a blush of blue;

this is the wind
  which rattled the weary windows
    in rooms of loneliness;

this is the wind
  that carried the scabious seed
    to its place in the meadows.

Is the wind good?
Is the universe good?
am I good?

What can one say? –
we are just ourselves:

I am myself,
the universe itself,
and the wind –
is the wind.

Ian M. Emberson

MOMENT OF LIGHT

There is a moment, again and again
(we hardly notice, we cannot find time)

when the clouds far off part, accidentally,
(it all depends on where we are standing and if

our eyes are lifted) and there is a white fall,
a poured radiating of slow still light

that touches a hill, a crown of elms, beyond us
imperceptibly and we step aside from our lives

for a moment – as when the spirit leaves the body –
(though we hardly notice, we cannot find time)

and we say nothing but (where does it come from?) become
graced and limitless ourselves, ourselves a moment of light.

Trevor Innes

KALEIDOSCOPE

I am in love with broken things
Prams once in use, their ribs all
Stuck out sideways, derelict,
And cars piled high and quite forgotten
Their huge eyes staring insect-like
And leaping in their nightmare lust
As if the moth-dust pampering
Must have its fill of rust at length;
And see these broken cups, have they
Not human tea-grief on the floor
Who once poured out an afternoon's
Convivial leafy offering?
Go search the poor, the odd, the maimed,
The useless ones who bear the ache
Of loss, they have a gift denied
The whole and never marred, the wide
Of fields still stranger to the rake;
These broken, random, ugly shards,
These ill-starred naked shoddy wastes
In these you find the harmony
Of castaways, past feeling, dry
And half-content with agony,
Discarded, save you see them whole
In the kaleidoscope bowl
Tap, tap and what a symmetry
Beyond design, and what reward
For pain and the often-fractured word.

S.L. Henderson Smith

WRONG NUMBER?

Still no reply –
God knows I've tried.
A voice keeps on repeating:
'The number you have dialled
is unobtainable. Please try later.'

Perhaps he's moved?
Gone ex-directory?
Could I have pressed the mute?

My neighbour
has no trouble getting through:
her God sits with a cordless telephone,
just waiting for her calls;
she says he's never out at all
what's more, he isn't bored
by all her chat. What could be
more miraculous than that?

Her God recycles her opinions
wraps them up in sweetie papers
– she calls them 'Guidance' then
and sucks them all the time
but I get whiffs of peppermint
and think they may be humbugs.

He's always at her church:
she won't let him attend
the other ones, although I know
he pops off on the quiet
when she can't see.

I've spoken to the engineers:
they say communication's privatised.
If I insist that I must share a line

there's very little they're prepared to do.
it's just I'd really like to know...
My God, where are You?

                                        Mary Sheepshanks

and said you

and said you all that glisters is not gold
that what we see is real or else a dream
that offers are not always what they seem
that far too late we learn what we were sold
that breezes soft and fragrant may turn cold

and in this coming eon will a plough
with constant pointers show a polar star
where i can always hitch my wandering car
or shall i sit beneath the apple bough
and casting out illusion find a tao

while time along his ever-rolling stream
re-churns our past and future scar on scar
and never can our tale be fully told
unless we pause in the eternal now

                                        Jim Kempster

REALITY EFFECT

Everything is happening today.
The sun is a mile high and light
is bouncing off the eucalyptus tree
at incredible speeds, the wind is
caught in two minds now there is
no more rain to manoeuvre, and
the sky has broken off its pow wow
with the clouds and sits alone
at the other side of the hill.
                            To a dog's eye
the scene creeps intuitively into focus:
the cut lawn, the magnolia and hawthorn,
the blue tit churring in the silver birch,
that stinking cat. Humans know things too:
the precise positioning of a leaf;
the pleasures of frogspawn;
the reason why, from a distance,
black and white cows in a green field
appear numinous shades of blue.

                            It's all
happening. Words are describing things,
telephones are ringing, next door's dog
yaps at the heap of flies busy-bodying
around bin bags and potato peelings –
oxygen is starving in a welt of CO
and greenhouse gases, while lightless attics
curse the foisty damp, the photographs curling,
the cobwebs, frisbees and frazzled Christmas trees.

Things-in-themselves waver like steel
on the quivery human compass;
you can feel the foundations tremble
as you drink your tea. We have no recourse
but to write, list after list, to get it all down
and fill in the gaps before the light
and the leaves and the park benches
and all the children playing on the grass
go hypoglycaemic and melt
back into the wordless and infinite regress...

It wasn't always like this. Yesterday
everything was happening somewhere
else. Take the cuckoo, for instance,
or the sound of a jet pursuing its own trail of spit
in the sky, or even the clinkety-clink
of ice in a tumbler. Tomorrow
everything will be different again.

Andrew Boobier

snow-line

Death is the solitary visitor whose
name you know. Below the
snow-line, glimpse tracks of
hares. We carry the burdens of our
hopes and cares upon our backs.
You speak as if edicts of desert-
tribes controlled your heart. You utter
prayers in a language you can not
impart. Enough sand has fallen through
that glass since Ishmael bruised his
heel and water flowed. Behind brown
eyes fear of the unknown grows.
Memories in the heart run slow.

We turn from pathways few
will tread. A harvest-field bred
faith above cracked clay. A rock
sheared by ice and glacial-melt
hid simple dreams. Nothing
is what it seems. The dead travel
fast. The past careens clouds above
tree-tops when leaves lie still.
Who finds truth within a bed
covered by a blanket woven
for merchants who could shelter you ? We
paint the years as icons. Sand
runs through the glass. I once played knuckle-
bones in the desert with Sharif Nasir in the
Wadi Araba, thirty years past.

Construct a heart from droplets of moisture
upon white tiles. Steam conceals
intention. Eyes framed by Burma
and by Gujarat, dance within opaque
light. Water swirls. My words

are an offering of care. Days pass. An exercise
of dreams enfolds the air. Outside, light-rain
graces the night. Car
headlights pass along the road. Jet
hangs on branches and in the
trunks of trees not yet bereft.
Birth is the gateway that your
senses seek. All in a week of watching
from the dark.

Robert Williams

ASANA

The man, who put his foot into his mind,
Had been trying to unwind
At a local Yoga class.

It was a somewhat unusual pose,
He was balancing on both elbows,
With one foot near his ear.

His aim was to impress,
But, in one moment of stress,
His foot slipped through

There was nothing he could do –

He was being swallowed
Body into mind, leaving behind...

An empty mat,
A surprised Yoga teacher.

Linda Marshall

CANDLES

Timid flames
ducking each draught of air,
taut flickers
jesting with oxygen,
waft-fleeing voiceless,
alcoved waifs
bracing gusts
strong as a gale-slam door:

I approach – the living light the dead –
pick you up,
blue collar, pallid face,
tip-light birth,
your sibling breathes your life
flame flame flame
light to light to light.

Cathedral's paid:
you join the spool of fire.
Human's crouched,
clenched from pew to pew.
Living now,
lit by the flaming dead,
watching now
one of the dead alive -

nostrils catch
the burnt scent of a death,
nostrils catch
the flickered smell of life.
My body
will navigate grey noon
but joins first
flittered mind, unthinking flame.

                                        K. E. Smith

RESTORATION

Wet, blown, temples cloven by the cold
Gasping with strife against the gust of wind
We sought to snatch a calm space in a turbulent day
And arrived at the Minster, late for Evensong.

We dipped through the low, dark door into the porch
And dripped, stunned by the sudden tall silence,
Feeling a warm relief – and then, the shock –
'It's closed. They're recording.'

Softening, he allowed us to sit in the nave,
Still, under surveillance, making no sound,
To share as outsiders, separated by the screen,
A secret audience to the action we could not see.

The sonority of the organ, the thin reed of song
Sometimes rose up above the storm – no words,
No meaning, but a distilled sensation seeping
Through the frenzied flap of polythene on the west wall.

But the sight of the height of the spring of the arch,
The sweep of gold light on the line of the vaults,
The shapes of the saints ranked in red on the screen,
The green glow of cloth, our small size in the shadows

Suffused the mind with such a sense of scale
That the deep crescendo of the roar that grew
And tried to shake this place, drowning man's voice
Could not move the stillness that we had found.

Sheila Bielby

THE WHOLE TRUTH

Perishing with loneliness
The whole truth
Slipped through a crack
Where cement became sand and ran out,
Wound herself round and round
Stairs leading to the council flat,
Seeped into little rooms.

Whole truth lives
In the rumpled sheets, the
Blankets thrown on the floor, the
Folded cardboard, the
Bills jammed together.
Whole truth sticks to the marmalade pot.

Nothing but the truth
Told her tale as
Milk turned solid in the tepid bottle
And shrouds of dust stuck to the grease.
Out of the rucked-up wardrobe contents
She makes her body,
She dribbles illicit puddles that miss the pan.

Where are you, whole truth?
Where do you live?
Do all the account books contain you
And the creases of newspaper?

Whole truth, come down from that ledge.
We love you. We die for you every day.
We do our damndest to spell you out,
For you count crumbs in account books,
Lay hands on you in all the angles of dust,
And before you, Your Worship,

Your Honour,
My Lord,
Cry or scream or
Have nothing at all to say.

Clare Chapman

TRUTH

Ultimately there is truth only in simple statements:
in Autumn the leaves fall; I love you; we shall die.
Ultimately there is comfort only in simple actions:
the impulsive caress, laughter, the urge to cry.

Really we long to give one gift, and only
hope for a simple exchange; but man has made
his life a twisted tower, where indirectly
he wanders proudly and vainly, or cowers afraid.

There was a road to joy once, but ingeniously
we constructed a maze, forgetting to keep the plan.
Heard voices cannot be traced now: inevitably
we have established the loneliness of man.

Can you not hear, laughter to which I listen,
how in my deathly corridor I cry,
asking for simple action by simple statement,
'In Autumn the leaves fall. I love you. We shall die'?

Brian Merrikin Hill

TERRACES

The all-devouring grave of constant earth
Is marked with terraces,
With Iron-Age ridges on the down, the mound
And strong-hold fields' perimeter.

A generation took up stone and flint,
Fought over tough ground, dug and smoothed it out,
Broke up the clods and hoped for springing green.
The tribes are buried by oblivion.

Sheep fray the edges of the vanished farms,
A cloud covers heights where sometimes hikers ramble,
A lizard wriggles abruptly in the sun,
A drowse of small yellow flowers.

Many-revolving billions of spheres
Flare over earth and seem to be eternal.
The neat small rows, the start of our collective,
Seem to be transient and are eternal.

Feathers of wheat break up the winter famine.
Look down through portholes in our noisy sky
At empty battlefields, winnings long abandoned,
Traces of terraces subduing earth.

Clare Chapman

EGGS

The egg clutch grabbed at my heart,
oh, there,
laid in a litter of brown bracken stalks and dried leaves,
visible,
but enough camouflaged for a foot to tread on,
full, rounded treasures,
nestled, clustered,
each one touching another,
complete in itself.

I'd read somewhere in Hardy, I think,
of a woman putting an egg in her bosom to hatch it.

If they'd survive,
what the bird was,
weren't questions to bother me
with them laid bare at my feet,
like jewels,
troubling my thoughts,
puzzling my mind,
catching my heart.

John Walker

THE HERDWICK RAM

As I unlatched the barn door's creaking hasp,
The grey ewes gathered, hungering, at my back,
Dawn's sallow glimmer pricked the tine and cusp
Of hawthorn crowns and slipped across the beck.
He wasn't in the clamour for fresh hay,
Nor by the mistle, so I went to seek
Hurrying through the damp grass, till I saw
The great, slumped shadow against the lambing creep.

A rim of light, pale cuticle of day,
Peeled back the shroud of night and, naked, trembled
About his corpse. The scavenging jackdaw
Retreated where the briar thickets scrambled
Down the banking to the weedy waters.
I knelt beside him in the soft churned mire,
Clasping the thick, coiled horns, whorled tortuous
As giant ammonites, and pulled him clear.

Thirteen winters toiling on the fells
Had earned him old age in the lower pasture,
And easy forage from the brimming pails
Of plump, flaked barley; shelter, a placid cluster
Of shearling ewes. He thrived for two more years
Before his withering heart curled like a leaf
And snapped its sinewy stem. Caught unawares,
Hot tears sprung, overwhelming me with grief.

Beneath the rowan tree we dug a pit,
No knacker's hacking blade to slit and skin
The heathery fleece, or spill the ripening gut
In heavy slicks, no splintering of bone
Against blunt cleaver. The sharp spade sliced the turf.
The rowan, giving up its dappled greens
For brief fire, spilled a russet blaze of leaf
And blood-spot berries across the earthy wounds.

The grey ewes move like shadows down the slope,
Blue smoke, straight up, from ashed and riddled fires,
Dogs bark, the wild, black geese reclaim the lake,
A cockerel's cry eviscerates the air.

Lesley Quayle

Ivy Leaf, Ian M. Emberson.

DEAD FOX AT THE FARMS' END

They hung the long red fox, like a flag, head-down
Out of the dead tree bent by the moor-squalls,
To show that the steep hard fields high beyond town,
    Still fought, from their humped walls.

Six young magpies, two gulls and a crow
Kept him company, swinging strung on a line:
Shots and the weather had tattered them, to and fro;
    Their wings had lost the shine.

But he still glowed alive with the sinking skies;
The wind scarce stirred him, heavy of muscle and bone.
Killed with a snarl, his open teeth and his eyes
    Struck the last of the sun

While women, in the damp beleaguered farms,
Looked out where the tall fox loomed with the dying light,
And shivered, drawing the blinds with thin white arms
    That could never shut out the night.

Ian Dewhirst

THE MEETING

The mid-November morning mist
blisters from the scrubby moor and fields
around the old fat factory,

the sun is a sliced lemon frozen in its own juice, as
just beyond the gates of the municipal tip
I pass a slow-moving lorry fill of aggregate.

Hard-pressed to brake, a young deer
lopes like an overgrown buck rabbit
across the road in front of me.

Offering not so much as a sideways glance,
it shrugs off the advancing steel of the car
with a singularly determined indifference.

I watch its curt white flash of arse
scoot into the roadside undergrowth
and then it is gone.

Were I a Pompeian soothsayer
or the Delphic oracle,
I would call such moments, *auspicious*.

But I am in middle-management,
mindful of a proposal I have to present
in Manchester this morning

for a particularly important client
whose name, for the time being,
escapes me.

Andrew Boobier

THE HARE

I'm an arctic ghost, now figure,
now ground, a shiver
on the white horizon;

a fierce and cunning mother,
I bear bone-aching cold,
a tenth of a life each gestation;

teach my young by secret visits
to found their form snug as skin:
each tastes my elixir for five minutes
before I freeze again with the sun.

Yes, I am white as the foot of the Virgin,
eyes set on heaven;
my children, melancholy,
drink my songs in darkness.

But I have two faces, two dances to wrong-foot
the gods. I scurry, a shadow, carrying wild
grasses to those they would see die.

Chris Bousfield

HOSPITAL STARLINGS

This place has all the concrete face
Of present time, no ivy softenings
No clumsy lines, nothing to blunt the craze
For razor edge and ruler sharpness here,
Allows no tears, no frowns, no doubts
To mar the pristine picture of our cleverness
And hides reality behind a mask;
There is a courtyard even so within –
A solitary tree left idle has a task
Incongruous in its benign simplicity –
To shelter starlings, silly, restless specks
Of black and purple; each gathering dusk
They chatter in language from another world
Bring music from the fields, the woods
To vitalise our cold modernity;
In them I hear old nature's beating heart
Again, renewed as by the falling of sweet rain
Swelling the earth and humanising pain
Making this elephantine hospital a place
Where bird song lives and throngs the healing air.

S.L. Henderson Smith

ROOK FLIGHT AT EVENING OVER FARNLEY MOOR

Always you wait till continents of cloud
from mainland mass to fractured isles have lent
their wilting pink, as if they held a proud
dominion over day's relinquishment;
then, through the glow of dusk's uncertainty,
when sun delves down to hibernate in night,
you taunt the fallowed fields' cold lethargy
with all the black-winged tumult of your flight –
rising from naked twigs – each dot a star
in an approaching galaxy. Then wings
spring from each dot, and suddenly the far
ocean of dusk with rook-cawed rioting rings,
as birds on birds, with clashing ebony cry,
eclipse that flamed fantasia of sky.

Ian M. Emberson

KINGFISHER DAYS

An electric flash of unexplained delight
– a kingfisher moment – streaked across my day
like blue-green rockets torched on bonfire night.
Where did it come from? Why? I cannot say.

When Turner dreamed of painting storms at sea
or mixed his palette for the *Téméraire*
did he recall a Yorkshire memory
of walking by the Washburn valley, where

he must have seen a feathered shaft of light
explode above dark waters, felt the thrill
of unexpected colour flood his sight,
and held his breath, heart-stopped, on heathered hill?

Kingfisher days grow scarce. I watch and wait:
send me one more – before it is too late.

Mary Sheepshanks

KINGFISHER DAYS

MARY SHEEPSHANKS

Cover design for *Kingfisher Days*, Mary Sheepshanks,
1998, Graham Rust.

ROSA CANINA

Sister, this year you have lost your shyness.

I have seen you waving at trains,
chatting with the hawthorn,
your rose cheeks
tipped towards the sun
in a perfumed arpeggio.

I have seen you too
leaning over ponds and lakes
holding a low note softly,
entering your own reflection, curious,
unafraid of the pike.

You are right to examine yourself,
to open out and know
your jewelled centrepiece.
Hold confidence
for you are beautiful.

Now, in a slow waltz you turn
down summer lanes, drink
chaliced wines in communion fields.
In coming out, you make it known to me,
that you are the wild rose.

Pat Borthwick

BLUE-DROP

You crouch, a form of prayer
over some mean flower
others have trod unnoticed.
Face buried in grass,
knees, elbows stained,
you stoop too low for sanity,
a man Gideon would not want,
beside you the Wild Flower Key
or the third Collins guide
worn out in ten years.

The meadow is alight,
blazons of yellow, red, purple.
But you search the quizzical,
plants that disguise
their signature of leaf,
pattern of petal, sepal.
They tease with games of I Spy
that switch to crossword puzzle,
binding grief-sown obsession
with the kindest of tendrils.

Back home, you know a bank,
spurge, sanicle in a green shade,
where in April bluebells glow.
You keep a snapshot,
your son against that blue,
a day no scars on show
yet a man seeded with demons.
For you, who watched him sink,
a place of consolation,
for him, a requiem glade.

For Michael E.,
Los Picos de Europa

Simon Currie

from PUGNEYS CHRONICLE:

OCTOBER

The ghosts are pressing again.
They take the air
from the lungs of the living.
They do it when bonfires singe
the beginning of Winter.
Though even Spring
has stirred to the foot on the stair,
a skirt, billowing a draught
in a door-shut room.

In the kitchen last night
they were pressing again.

The house lost its tongue.

On the wall,
the brass-bevelled box
vibrated its glass,
all six of the small striped flags
signalling
summons:
from the Master's Dressing room
Madam's Bedroom, Sewing room,
Parlour, the Nursery
especially the Nursery –
all the bells
pressing.

                                        Josie Walsh

AFTER MEDITATION

It was a robin's song
that pierced the tangled afternoon
with its sharp, sweet wisdom: –
'Beneath this knotted earth
there is summer
– inside your troubled mind
there is peace'.

'Why is Spring so long in coming?'
I asked the sage in the tree.

– But the bird had gone.

                                        Catherine Emberson

SNOWPRINT

Faint but perfect,
The feathered impression of grouse wings
In the blank snow of the moor,
The take-off moment printed.

I turned for the photograph:
One of my boot clumps had clipped a wing.

It would not have lasted, anyway,
This print of white on white,
So light the impression where
Air kissed earth goodbye.

                                        John Walker

OCTOBER FALL

Light and lifted, spirit of the air
dancing in my hair: a thousand
leaves swirling down the sway
of lackadaisical lanes, under
the webbed skylights of tall oaks,
echoes of burnt summers crinkling,
raw siennas ready to fall
and join the grand autumn whirl.

Strolling, I stray through the lower
rooms of breeze, down the generous
river hip of a road, deeper and deeper
into hazel browns and skittish golds,
flurries of ochre and red hula-hooping –
mild, wild October celebrating itself;
'peach of a weather, like no tomorrow'.

                                        Linda Marshall

I KNOW IT LIVES IN GREENHOUSES

I have sought it out.
Its still centre breathes soft
with the cucumbers
against the sloping glass.

Through the clanking of boiler pipes
the lighting of paper cones
it does not bat an eye. Is cool.

If I lived there
amongst the erratic twitch of greenfly
I would go mad.
I would hear roots slurp,
shoots stretch to grasp
at bamboo poles and twine,
flowers knock their heads
on the window-panes.
I could not be at ease.
Or I would hear silence,
enough to know the music
of my own stem-blood rising,
and be afraid.

And yet to visit here,
to enter this glass temple
is to believe and be.

I have found it too
in an empty swimming pool,
a deep bowl, a stone.
Simply there. Still as moss.
A stillness balanced
between sound and silence.

Pat Borthwick

A VISIT TO SÈTE
(Le Cimetière Marin)

I stopped where Valéry must have stopped.
I stopped to read his poem just as he
Might have read a poem by Mallarmé.
The breeze turned the pages; I turned my head;
I turned to turn with him as he turned,
Just as he was no more than a turning
Because it was natural to turn,
To think of other poets who have turned,
Will surely turn because turning is
What poets do.
Poets turn and climb; they burn in the sun,
Climb these terraces to the Phare St. Clair
Whose crescent of light at night inspires what
But shock? I do not know what I reap
Except a desire to reap more than sense.
Wordless interjections hang in the air,
While the sea ushers in the final
Songs of the Sirens' misterioso...
Ecstatic O's long drawn out affirm
A current of song wordless and yet
Full of meaning, absolute meaning,
The absolute music of the sea.
The gift of life has gone into the grasses,
Dropped carelessly like a paper tissue.
I finger the tomb; the words sing...
O récompense après une pensée
Qu'un long regard sur le calme des dieux.

Sète (Hérault) Summer 1967

Gordon H. Dyson

ORCHARD SHIPLEY

Counterfeit wedding bells
Blossom never to fruit,
Gusted pink confetti
In a Shipley wind.

Lifted striped market shoppers
an invasion of bedazzled dust
A fondling summer's warning and
                    eyed, hooved and erect,
A sudden squall: 'kerchiefs, tents
Far back as Agincourt billowing
And camel, goat, bag out.

The accident of a late spring Fall.
No painter, Manet, no Seurat, and
Mothers through a veil embarrassed
                    smiling,
Forgotten like the rest of us in
                    weddingtint.

Misted girls from Woolworth undressed laughter
Flamingos
And through record sleeves
Magnolia.
Blossom there is everywhere
Blossom and no fruit.
Shipley.
Oh such impossible cherry
And such out of date virginity.

                                        Neville Hodgson

**'West Riding', from _Three Brontë Poems, 1993_,
Ian M. Emberson.**

WAKING TO THE WATERFALL OF LIGHT

I am a tree, with
eyes of cloud-drift,
arms flowering into air.
My feet root for ageless
water. Saplings surround me.
There – see the birds
flitter from my heart
and hair. The dark
sidles round me. I'll wake
to the same place, its breezes,
awash with dappling light.

Trevor Innes

SUNLIGHT AND WIND ON LANTY'S TARN

                                        – I feel drunk
astride this mossed and oxide silver trunk
that's scaled and patched with lichen, the crinkled dross
on melted lead. The tree I'm on leans out and dips –
lap lip lap as wrinkled ripples slop
their brilliant drops. I look into the wind
which flings handfuls of gold coin in my face.
I wince and blink and close my eyes.
I feel the whole trunk twist
beneath me in the torque of wind.
I hear the rush of pine and spruce, the rasp
of scratchy bracken, the hiss
of little twisting yellow leaves of birch.
I look up – zig-zag snags of twigs, still disced
with tarnished sixpence leaves – more saw-toothed hearts –
I look down – reticulated veins of light
snake and braid in ravelled skeins, casting their net,
scale under-water stones like fish. I stare
where light's unlookable
          where wind and sun and water flare.

                                        Nicholas Bielby

CONFESSIONAL

I want a poem like a Chinese box
riddled in seamless ivory, such that
it is a thing to pause and wonder at –
not true nor false, a Cretan paradox;
or where, within a world of backward clocks,
smoke, gathering to a chimney, gushing down
to incandescent ash, lights flames which then
in-fold, re-member limbs and loins and locks;
not good nor bad, as deeds or likenesses
or knives are good and bad; as Sato's blade
was good that shivered light and nerve: well-made,
not for its use, but in itself; that has
the svelteness of a tool evolved to free
boxes in-folded in the ivory.

                                            Nicholas Bielby

FOR WILLIAM CARLOS WILLIAMS 1883-1963

you looked at the world
and it was
new

your words
point
to the ancient journey

we've all made to survive
time and make
our lives

you sympathize
with what we use
and show wounds

inflicted
everywhere
we act

sometimes we heal
each other
but with the planet now conquered

and a new world
contrived
we watch

with all our power
your new world
die

Fred Schofield

THE SMITHY AT HAWORTH

Bright from the fire, the iron glows
on the anvil. So, tipped with light,
the black bar's a spear would sear
the jelly of an eye. Flakes fall from it,
passive under the hammer blows.
    It takes shape. The elements
    of fire and violence,
disciplined to making something, meet here.

The smith tells me wrought iron was
first a hobby; but, he explains,
after five years he's made the grade;
now he is free to make his own designs,
and makes a living. One would guess
    his beard is consciously
    mid-nineteenth century.
He works Sundays to catch the tripper trade.

He's forged his freedom, having made
his craft his trade. It's hard to find
where energy and action meet
in making things of any truth or kind
before the sullen glow can fade.
    And that is more than I,
    a Sunday passer-by,
can do, who warm myself at his hearth's heat.

Nicholas Bielby

DEATH OF A CRAFTSMAN
(In memory of Harry Pennington)

Let him go easily,
the old man,
slide smoothly
from the launch-pad into death.
He who so loved
to make and to maintain
has finished now
with his hard-worn and battered frame.

He lost three fingers once
– they were expendable he said:
his other hand became
more skilful for the loss.
He stood, wind-proofed,
against life's buffeting –
indigenous as oak and ash and thorn.

To watch him carve a chair,
mend clocks or paint a room
was to feel all the rhymes and metres
flowing right.
His tools were inspiration,
in his hands they sang invention.

Let him go starwards fast,
his spacecraft spirit
fired by the rocket of his finished life:
the motor has burned out
and can be jettisoned
at last.

Let him go easily.

                                        Mary Sheepshanks

From HINDEMITH: CONCERTO FOR ORGAN, 1962

(First public performance, Lincoln Center, New York
1962; Conductor, Hindemith.

ALLEGRO

it goes on
Your breakfast is served
Life retains its hum-drum reality
But there's a stirring in the air
Ah Hindemith they knew you well
those who perceive
the chords in the air, not yet cut,
nor yet surmised
No awareness of scissors,
the sharpness is an octave higher
There's life in the magic still
Who knows where it leads?
Beneath the city
the subway carries its herd
of commuters
The traffic
sits waiting
for the red to change to green
as amber flashes

Gerald England

ARABESQUE

like to
an ankle-winged
messenger touching down
lighter than air

balance
on one leg
t' other extended
pointing backward
forward inclined trunk
arms outstretched in one sinuous
line flowing front to rear

silently
gracefully
undetected
wrestle with
laws of nature
support whole weight
on point of one mighty toe
encased in pretty builder's boot
nail dropped off from bruising
or surgically removed
how many pascals
are clobbering
bone and
flesh at
the ex
trem
it
y

not to worry
arabesque does not
require this every time
pointe is the painful mode
the other two are easier

hang on
arabesquing men
always do *plante* or *demi-pointe*
pointe is only ever performed
by women

nul point aux hommes

Jim Kempster

ALL FOR A POINT

– Bradford City v. Coventry City,
Carling Premiership, November 1999

From where we sit, left side of Midland Road,
the view up Valley Parade, topped by Belle Vue,
gives hints of Bradford's story. Drab workshops
mark the left. Uphill a one-time seedy pub,
converted to Islam, is now a venue
for sober men to meet. T.A. barracks
hide on a dead-end street. Low November
sun seems out of place. A heartening home win's due.

Players run on. An outsize Kop cranks itself
into full voice, less bel canto than gruff.
Opening moves unsettle us, by-pass
a disarmed defence. Coventry's first approach
rounds off with the simplest of goals, enough
to stun three sides of the ground, a bludgeon
to well-nursed hopes. The fight back is urgent,
measured in grit. City's resolve becomes tough.

By half-time it's one all, both teams pushing
for the lead, chances at each end, a clash
of two sharp edges carving out canny
attacks or parrying others away.
All this is played for higher stakes than cash,
for each city's name and sense of itself,
a purpose beyond the visible graft
of two sides cutting their brave athletic dash.

Second half. No further score, but close shots
are fired both ways. Strikers hit bar, side net,
defensive wall; keepers on red alert;
midfield duels providing eddies of art
in a shifting game. Bradford's massed choirs let
loose their volleys of faith: 'City till I die'
pours down tiers and rows, overflowing the pitch.
A single point. There's hope of survival yet.

John Cook

PALETTE

(based on the life and work of Vincent Van Gogh)

Potato eaters
  earth to earth in tones of brown
    you give them re-birth.

Sunflower madness
  scattering seeds of despair
    on yellow canvas.

Starry, starry night
  restless landscape inky blue
    trees flare and moon burns.

Black crows hovering
  fatal corn and troubled skies
    your soul is laid bare.

Catherine Emberson

THE NIGHT CAFÉ: VINCENT VAN GOGH, 1888

Drinkers slump in corners, harsh lights
dazzle above a monstrous table;
a man in white watches.
Bilious yellow – the nausea of night
caught in swirling strokes...

The image is familiar.
Reduced to postcard respectability,
it lurks on gallery shelves, coffee tables,
examination rooms, yet still it shocks.
Biographies give time and circumstance

but do not prepare for such casual,
commonplace despair. The floor escapes
its frame, sliding towards us. A clock
is fixed forever at twelve fifteen a.m.
Most of us have passed a night here,

though in other cities, other times.
Even in faded print, Vincent's nightmare
touches ours. Stare, and dimensions blur,
until we, too, plunge towards that gaping,
curtained, room beyond.

                                                    Pauline Kirk

JEAN ARNOLFINI AND HIS WIFE, PAINTED BY JAN VAN EYCK

1.
These two stand in their narrow room;
  five hundred years they've waited thus:
her hand in his, one on her womb,
  his right hand raised, dismissing us.
They would take off their fancy dress:
  his outsize hat, her grave-green gown:
lie naked on that bed and kiss,
  but they are never left alone.
Intruders in the convex glass
  keep children from their grownup game
of love and marriage, playing house:
      Why don't the guests go home?
Outside the window, in clear light,
ripe cherries beckon birds to bite.

2.
Illusions, durable through centuries,
  projected by a magic-lantern mind,
enchanted into paint's paralysis,
  you wait to be let speak, or drop a hand.
Young sir, well disciplined by staid attire,
  responsibility's absurd black hat
snuffs out your animal, spontaneous fire,
  if your pale face be capable of that.
She doesn't look into your lashless eyes
  but futureward; beneath her gown's green fold
a child's child quickens. This anonymous
deathbound manvessel, in voluminous
  green garments, may already sleep in mould,
so, standing still, the masked lay-figure lies.

                                        Anna Adams

FRAMED
(*that* picture, Van Eyck)

Her gown is green,
the kind of green not often seen
indoors and much less
on a wedding dress:
the kind of green that startles
 on an April morning after rain,
the green of fields in sudden sun,
of budding hawthorn leaves, of birth,
of growth, the green of
teeming, green of health –
and come to that,
the green of wealth.

His gown is brown, or puce
as are his eyes –
the purple-brown of peat
through thinning heather,
the brown of careful husbandry,
the brown of money, study, heirlooms –
and of the darkest corners of the room
they're painted into.

Her skin is cream,
the cream of statuary,
the cream of parchment
yet to be inscribed,
the cream of luxury,
the cream of dreams.

The bed is red, the red of embers,
the furnishings the red of blood
and their hearts –
as her eyes, pupil-black,

look past his left hand
neither claiming nor relinquishing
her own, not offered nor withheld
and past his right,
neither inviting nor denying
guests their time,
their centuries –
their hearts are colours
we can only guess.

Julia Deakin

DIAMOND

Glistening drop of water-rock
singing of past sun
captive in you.

Your brilliance was obscured
by ages of stone.

Gem-brightness now
freed by craftsman's skill
to pierce, reflect, adorn.

Christine England

EDVARD MUNCH SETS UP HIS EASEL.

Little, shrunken, pallid sister
Skin pulled so taut over skull
Inside sockets roll fevered eyes
I give blood-red, fortifying wine
See, see it go down
I can trace its course down her gullet,
My stranger, my translucent subject
I give up my months to your capture

Poor soul, beached there on the tumbled bed.
Must heave her upright, prop her up with cushions
Papa, elder sister settle and soothe
Soothe, soothe...
In the doorway servants and relatives
Look, they whisper and cluck
They're all in black
Their hair is all scraped back
They fold their hands before them
clasp and unclasp.
Ooh, the poor, poor thing
You can tell

No tolling yet. Open a window or two
Let Spring in
Sister needs a whisper of the world
See her eyes turn sunwards
Slowly they turn

Now maintain that pose. That one's good
Keep still. Hold that hand outflung
You lot freeze. Habitual postures.
You more to the left. Papa that bending over her.
The eyes burn, the hair is bodiless
Ivory, every shade of grey for that head
Scrape, scrape, for the bone under that skin
Trace line by line the courses fever takes
You flat ground show dimensions of the wraith

Stare, stare, by mornings by months
Leech-like suck, slowly devour, slowly take in
I love you, girl. I love you crumpled
Barely alive
I'll force those others' loves
Before this canvas they will lift their hats
Before this canvas they will stop they will sigh
As if they were in church
They'll love you they won't deny me.
Before the bright blood bursts,
White girl, turn your eyes to sunlight.

This mania is a fever to enliven you
It is my stare that fixes you for ever.
Before I rot, before my face drops from the bone,
Before I'm forgot
Watch how I fix
Scrape. Stare. Scrape.
Devour and fix.

Clare Chapman

'it's not what we sent you to college for'

I called you Laurence Stephen – a plain enough name
I thought, but dignified – and prayed
that some day you'd be an artist
like Dante Gabriel Rossetti.

Dante Gabriel Rossetti, now there was a name
to conjure with – and yes, he conjured goddesses.
Full throated creatures, larger than life
who filled the canvas with a sigh
that left you breathless –

but what have you done? What do you paint
larger than life? 'A mass of humanity'? A mess.
Your figures hump-backed, scurrying, bent double...
daren't they stand up straight, your men?
Layabouts, dogs and grim
hags at people's backs, like death.

I paint what I see, mother.

All these years I've waited for
a sign, one line of artistry –
and what have you given me? Smudges.
Spoil heaps. Rivers like cesspools.
Shiftless crowds. The eye directionless.
Not making sense of the world –

then maybe it doesn't make sense –

you could have done so well. You used to draw
but now you daub. You could have made your name, like
Dante Gabriel Rossetti – poetic and angelic –
now he could paint. Your landscapes sprawl.

You speak for yourself, mother.

I speak for millions, son.
And cripples! What do you paint them for?
Sometimes I don't know where to look.

Then why don't you look at me, mother?
Why don't you look at me?

Julia Deakin

CASSANDRA BURNING JANE

– Cassandra Austen, elder sister of Jane Austen, is believed to have burnt many letters that may have expressed overflowing feeling. Parts of the life of one of our greatest novelists, Jane Austen, are lost to us, but Cassandra felt she was fully justified on the grounds of propriety and sisterly love.

Now that I, flexing my grateful toes
Before hearthside flame –
How it glows –
Play my part: bonneted dame,
Toothless and tame,

Look at treasure I hold in my hand,
My privacy's hoard,
Oh ho, a whole band
Of scribes would sell a whole land
To be here where I stand.

I determine to make away
With secrets now mine. I hold the sway.
The vulgar, the idle, shall never divine
what precision, what force
was behind the burnt line.

Now sister, rest quiet as you burn,
as fires in rapacity lick, turn
you to ash.
Part of your soul as well
eludes the biographer's spell
in a flash, in a flash.

I, arbiter of her lives
Keep far from prying eyes
bits of her life,
free from the stupid lies,
lecturers' greedy cries,
vanity's strife.

Good wench. Let unenlightenment come,
Beat muffled drum.
Burn all that stuff. Commend you now.
Over this passion's glow
Veils, murk and ashes throw,
Cover that brow.

Clare Chapman

PATRICK AT HARTSHEAD

– One evening in April, 1812, soon after the unsuccessful
Luddite attack on Cartwright's Mill, Liversedge, the Rev.
Patrick Brontë was passing the churchyard on his way home
late at night when he was enraged to see men moving about
silently, in the darkness, on the other side of the wall. Then
he realised it was a Luddite burial, performed secretly in order
to prevent further arrests.

In the dwindling hours
between midnight and morning
gouging out rock,
one lamp at the head,
lower, yet slower,
square up the corner;
a coffinless body
needs depth for a bed.

A few quiet words
– was anyone listening? –
'Ashes to ashes
In certain hope' –
Only the bird
of warning calling
and the ghost of a whispered
'Amen!' from the road.

Nobody saw him,
or sensed he was there,
yet, later, he came
with fresh milk and bread;
his knock on the door,
his foot on the stair
and a silence of secrets
– shared! – at Hartshead.

Mabel Ferrett

BRONTË WAY

Was it like this then –
bog-cotton milk maids
purple and silver grass
a curlew's continual song
punctuated by sheep cries?
Did she stride uncaring
through boggy patches
in unsuitable shoes
lie face up to the sun
as I do now, eyes closed
friends' voices a murmur
behind a stone wall?
Did she seek her Spirit
giver of great poems
and one strange novel
on such high June
days brief in intense beauty
between the darkness.

Jean Barker

BRANWELLIANA

1. Luddendenfoot

Water glistens on the cutting wall
and sodden couch-clumps drop
driblets on the blackened soul:
Jesu, Jesu, lift me up.

The soul flaps from the Weavers Arms
to spirits at Lord Nelson's bar,
prophets of the worsted firms:
Jesu, Jesu, Salvator.

But slinks away from flooded peat,
from thigh deep swirls in Styx,
from barghest and bog-holes:
Jesu, Jesu, Jesu Rex.

Why there's room at every inn
for the soul to wink at hell,
for gold liquid and dark women,
Jesu, Jesu, slake me still.

2. Family Portrait

A pause, a paintstroke, he's brushed himself out
so his hands, his fine veins, his haunted face,
are not to be found in his family's frame
though he pales back to haunt the three who remain.

They are scattered against the backdrop now,
staring us out in this mutual puzzle –
how does four go into three leaving none?
They're looking through us to no avail.

Though all golden sections are four by three
and imbalance so maps a magic whole
the poise in this picture is rigid now –
with the tiniest tilt they'd swing to the side.

Only closing their eyes could refill their world
for they blench abrased at this blankness of us
As they struggle to re-envisage the life
he once painted in from his different place.

K.E. Smith

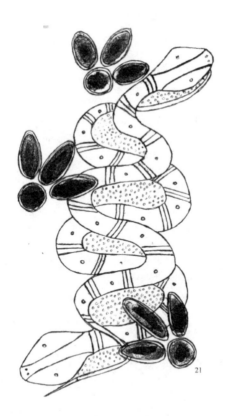

**Snake and Emu from *Return to Dreamtime*, 1996,
Pauline Kirk.**

LIFE'S LONE WILDERNESS

– Mrs Gaskell to a friend, Aug 1850, re Charlotte Brontë:
'She said...that I (Mrs Gaskell) had no idea what a companion
the sky became to one living in solitude – more than any
inanimate object on earth – more than the moors themselves.'

She watches from that lonely house
the narrative of sky –
the cirrus twisting in the wind
beyond the grouse's cry –

the changing clouds' companionship,
the flow of white and grey,
a random drama acting out
digressions to the day;

and flowing from her moving pen
a tale of two who yearn,
as one sail trembles on the winds
of exile and return –

returning to a waitful shore
beyond an ocean wide;
then, with that final word 'farewell',
her pen is laid aside.

Now fruits of evening ripen fast
(she fears the sleepless husk)
as one by one the moorland cloughs
fill with the tides of dusk.

Can she forget three flowers
which lie all wilted in the vase,
as sunset snails beneath earth's edge
and slimes the sky with stars.

Ian M. Emberson

WHAT WILL SURVIVE OF US

SURVIVORS

You had come round when we arrived,
survivors of a summer storm,
hailstones, flash floods, fork lightning.
I brought you strawberries,
their juice soiled your theatre gown.

When you arrived half a century ago
strawberry marked, I blamed
the midwife's clumsiness,
did not confess to nervousness
of a raging summer tempest.

Survivor of storms and strawberries
you joked about the stained gown,
blamed me for marking it yet
confessed to the preference
of sweet juice to spilled blood.

When more visitors arrived we left,
and drove back in evening calm,
the umbilical sun pulsing through
the hospital avenue, my guilty hands
stained with strawberry juice on the wheel.

Joyce Thornton

AT THANKSGIVING

Born prematurely – 'This small' –
the weight of the sugar bag
balanced in my father's palm.

I saw my mother's blanched face and you
nestled; clenched, unclenching
in your blue sleeping suit.

Frail fledgeling, I claimed you.
And you thrived, grew,
outstripped us all.

I follow your migrations
from the cramped quarters,
rooms you've occupied, always
a seasonal visitor.

I would weight you with gifts –
books, pictures – concerned
for what's left behind. You skim,
light in the updraught.

You slid out of sight
into the departure lounge, left us
pressed in the crush.

Crawling from the airport,
feeling for the bite of the clutch,
I roll down the window, strain
for the note of the engine.

(Strapped in, you sense
sun on a silver wing,
the belly lift, begin
the slow climb).

Postcards track your flight west.
At Thanksgiving you call, crow
you' ll settle – 'Almost married'
– so warm there – 'I dream of snow'.

Gliding in the wind, insouciant;
you cheat fate.
I give my thanks,
pack your winter coat.

Judith Bolland

MOTHER

I   Gifts

Swill it up, eyes down. Don't say a thing.
Keep it shut. These are my mother's gifts:
and when someone boasts
or says it's no big deal,
she lifts her eyes heavenward.
One day I'll be like her: it'll be easier.

II   Failed encounters

I'm sorry I never met you, Mother, face to face.
Sounds easy but we hardly ever got it together.
Though you never seemed to notice.

I'm sorry. We're not supposed to rhyme
with each other, you and me; best work
at maintaining our boundaries.
Which means edges.

Jenny's mother last Sunday in the nursing home,
mouthing her silent screams. We'd better go,
said Jenny and I agreed, get back to the land of the living.
Remember Filey? I ask her as we hurry away.
But what can you say in such circumstances?
Shoot me first, said Jenny.

III Grandson

He's in the family grave where she will go,
a grandson with dusky skin, cyanosed, slightly yellow
like her, a post-mortem cut to the head.

There's room for me, she said,
I bought it for five when Mother passed away,
not counting your baby. Two hundred pounds.
I didn't think that was bad?

IV Home

The shame of dying, of coming home
to that familiar place, looking out of the same face
as my mother, her ordinary face;

the shame of disappearing, a lost monument
grassed over, 'In Memory of my Mother' washed away,
her scattered flowers, broken stones.

Chris Bousfield

POEM FOR BRETT

'Yes, I will' ,
My mother's words carry her up the rainsloping hill.
'I will get my own'.
Yes, mother,
you want the greeting of yourself
the freshest hour.
You could snap your old bones,
the mist, the uneven climb
flowers twelve inches above your head, still climbing.
You call to me through the mist and the rain
'I'm coming down',
(your hands tinted with sweet peas).
Yes I have pride, and the hidden sun pumps my heart.
Proudly you are torn from me now, but a scent remains.
Your old age stumbled up the rainsloping hill for a posy;
Through the generations
'Congratulations', I call.

Joan Lee

MOTHER'S DEATH

What a night to die.
A summer's night, a lover's night.
The earth sings
And you die;
Never to see,
Oh, never to sense,
This
Again.

Up there in front and to either side
The trees tighten the already narrow steep-sided valley,
Behind, it greenly winds away to distantly admit
                          the jewel-eyed village,

Five tennis courts, a bowling green, a children's park,
                the clubhouse cover the valley-bottom.
Slight figures petal the small cleft of land.
Each come from winters to play
One night as Kings
Upon the surface of the earth;
There is laughter and song and rejoicing,

As it is with my foot on the ground I feel the earth alive,
So it was that night we made love in the garden.
The lilac was loving, the grasses sweet and tousling.
We laughed and were happy.
And every blade, and bird and stone,
Every tree and all the shadows were attendant.
And my mother dies tonight.

                                    Wendy Clayton

EGGSHELL

This room was his eggshell
where he incubated his illness
tucked into the settle bed
near the kitchen range.
He watched his mother kneading dough
crimping pastry - flour dusting her arms
and helped with srnall chores:
shelled peas, peeled potatoes
polished spoons and forks
until his arm ached.
His reward, a rosy pomegranate
secreted in the bread crock;
his pleasure as sharp as each segment
prodded out carefully with a pin,
firm kernels packed in fleshy fruit
brushing gently round the edges
sour and sweet, savoured on the tongue.

Josh would return soon
sapling thin, ironbar strong,
as he was not, with a present;
penknife, tin whistle or neckerchief
bartered at Newcastle Market.
After supper would clear a space
and work at the table
whittling willows, bending them into cages
ready to sell finches, sixpence a bird.

Josh entered, hung his cap
behind the door, 'ullo young 'un
close yon eyes. He waited
breathing halted, felt something
smooth and warm, spherical.

Keep it on yon chest. He lay still
egg nested in his ribs
beating his wings against the bars;
felt the vibration of gradual separation
of shell, sensed the chick's exhaustion
silently urged him on, squinting down
to have a closer look as the matted
heap of feathers tumbled free
dark eyes meeting and holding his own.

Margaret Speak

AT BETTY'S

The perspective of the silver teapot
At odds with the table; the amber sugar
In a circular dish that looks oval;
The peppermint tisane mellowing the mind
Like a mild, foreign cigarette; the two of us,
Sitting at a tangent, deeply distracted;
The silence between us, jarring
In the murmur of voices, mix of laughter;
The high romantic windows looking out
On huge snowflakes, swirling as if shaken –
But it is mid-May; the flurry is white
Cherry blossoms skidding on a cool wind
That signals change. We begin to talk...

Linda Marshall

SPOILED CHILD

I only knew one Grandparent.
The rest, all five, I thought
had worked themselves to death.

My Grandmother, she knitted;
swaddling clothes for a caterpillar child
who, coddled, bounced from Aunt to Aunt
in their spinster deference.

She knitted their relationships
set plain against the pearl
demanding righteousness from all.

She knitted from her Quaker stock
a vocabulary of 'thee's' and 'thou's',
list of sins - all unforgiving
many were quite spontaneous.

She knitted webs of intrigue with her neighbours,
who would leave me guessing
expecting warm embrace
but greeting me with their blank stares.

She knitted and I helped to wind the skeins
which were to make a lifelong coat of fear
a punishment, to do those good works
which she could never do.

She knitted my conception
of a Virgin Birth
found drifting in the bulrushes
or under a gooseberry bush.

Albert Thornton

JUMP!

I am a child planted on a path which curves away.
Ahead my parents, who just minutes ago held my hand
have let go, walked off and are leaving me.

I watch. They don't look back and I don't say –
don't want to know there's nothing I can do
to turn them round.

I'm on my own now, falling back through years
onto a kindly held out blanket – who holds that? –
of memories from which I bounce back up, up

onto my father's or my mother's shoulders, light enough
to ride there like a little empress with the wide world
                                                    at my feet
mine for the asking and the sun an outstretched hand
                                                    away.

But I grow – I grow too big and heavy for them,
weigh their strong young adult bodies down
as they must have their parents, groundwards.

Swaying, I look back down a tower of acrobats:
strong men and women who as their feet sank deeper into
                                                    clay
reached skywards with their children.

But I have none: no child to lift onto my shoulders
(or walk away from). Yet as their concentrated sinews
urge in me some *tour de force*

I look round for some high point I can jump to –
feel their voices rising through me – *Jump*, they're saying
and I'm saying *jump*, now –

Julia Deakin

SALLY JEROME, PAINTER, IN MEMORIAM
(1905-2002)

ON A FLY-LEAF:
'THE SUN HAS GOT HIS HAT ON'

I'm melting now into the sun's eye
all glinting-white, faceted as once
that complex harmony of your smile
between eyelid hoods and thinning lips

    Coo coo, coo coo, coo-oo-oo

A wood-pigeon startles as I flop
with no ice-creams now onto this bank –
It's the season for dahlias, you'd
note; and the sunflowers as they turn
keep an uncalculated faith.

See that dragonfly's spectacular
display, wings like shot-silk, dive-bombing
nothing; yes, a dance of certainties
rulers would give any body's brain for

    Coo coo, coo, coo-oo-oo

I squint my eyes towards 'our moors'
Sense your presence as in the fragrance
of these briar roses curling back
towards autumn: and the Red Doles' hollyhocks
we loved will soon be caught bending out and into
                    northern winds

    Coo coo, coo-oo-oo

So when the old woman shrouded
in layers silhouettes

with her stick against the year's eerier lights
my lips will redden as always to greet you
until, with no surprise, she turns, and turns about.

    Coo coo, coo-oo-oo

Only then, once the doors are locked, and bolted
Only then will it register truly
    'you' are gone:
No more odd messages through the door
Gone your easel from the window

I shudder - it's already a coat colder
here without you at my side
But, like the random flashes of my wood-notes
How could you desert me? never again visit, or ignite??

    Coo coo, coo-oo-oo-oo

Anna Taylor

AU SAINT SEVERIN

We do not meet here.
It is just a café among cafés.
It holds no meaning for us.
And yet there is a meeting.
I meet, for example, myself.
I meet, for example, the stone
So snugly embedded in the peach I cut
In remembrance of you. I slice away
Layers of receded selves like onion rings;
Who am I, black shirt, umbrella, no tie,
Peeling myself away to nothing?
The stone is now a symbol of
Love enclosed
In homes, out of reach;
The stone is now a symbol of
Loneliness exposed
On an untouched beach.
I buy another. I smile, asking myself
If one peach can contain two truths.
How many more, latent, lie in store?

Gordon H. Dyson

MEETING

And so we walked,
the platform's length.
You in your practised way
and I, afraid that you would know
how ill at ease I felt
how over-keen to keep your pace.

You collapsed the white stick like a magician's wand.
We talked old times, of mutual friends,
the snakes and ladders of our lives.
You never mentioned blindness.
And I was struck, not
by your unseeing eyes
but your white hair, cut so close
to skin I'd never seen before.
You made me laugh, as ever.
And your listening
disappeared the other passengers.

But how I wished we both had seen
the gypsy horses; clod-hopping, unsleek coats,
startled by our approaching train, their canter –
hoofs leaving the ground, manes flying,
heads half-turned to face us.

Josie Walsh

FRENCH CHALK

Every time she used the Linguaphone in class
Miss Withers remembered her student year in France..
The boy at her pension, her landlady's son
who brought coffee and croissants
to her room each morning before
he strode his motorbike and roared back to work
at the village boulangerie. She would have liked
to know him better, her secret longing
had only been fulfilled when one evening
after she had made her notes, she went
across the yard to the lavoir for her toilette
and he was bathing there, stripped down to his pale skin.
Her white blouse, loose about her
prim Englishness she pulled it and herself
together and could only murmur
'Pardon, vous m'avez étonné'.

Her girls were good at pronunciation,
the Linguaphone made sure of that.
But sometimes their tittering was
too much for her to bear, especially when
the place was reached where Madame
addressed her husband as 'cherie'
That was when her flat bosom
under her knitted twopiece, new each term,
palpitated as she saw the phantom
of her French landlady's son,
his skin opalescent in the moonlight,
the water splashes refracted into rainbows
and her inner voice uttering 'que je t'adore'
as she stripped her white blouse
from her slight form and with it
tenderly sponged his glistening back.

Joyce Thornton

INCOMPATIBLE

He could not stop buying rainbows.
She would pay anything for the stars.
There were rainbows on his combs,
His shirts, his sheets, his wristwatch.
She had a moon on her shoes, a star
On her scarf, constellations dangling
From her ears.

Rainbows for him were fleeting:
Psychedelic doorways blossoming
In a mixture of weather. But she
Admired the constancy of stars –
The hard glitter and glamour of
The night sky. A star could be
A diamond on her finger.

He once gave her a rainbow necklace.
She cried when its light faded.
There was fire and ice on his sleeves –
The starry cuff-links from her boutique.
His wrists hurt. He loved her as a lover
Of symbols. But rainbows and stars
Are like day and night.

Linda Marshall

PEACH AND GINGER

Unpacking her stuff,
she lends me *The Little Prince*
to flip through,
as she sets the speakers up,
works the leads around the table.

She puts on Miles Davis,
drapes a throw over the drab chair,
hands me a peach and ginger candle
and stands her saxophone
in the corner by the door:
a signature.

She hands me a peach
and ginger candle,
inviting me
to test its peach
and ginger fragrance.

Miles away,
I'm doubly mirrored
in the convex chrome
of her angle poise clock
reflected in the looking glass.

On ne voit bien qu'avec le coeur
She puts the candle on the shelf.
L'essential est invisible pour les yeux
She curls up on her quilt and puzzles
where to put her posters up.

Ed Reiss

FAUSTA: A NEW ALPHABET

Without a word
we trod the moor

Our steps sliding backwards
our rickety pasts.

Is this the place
where forests grew leaves

and glaciers rose
in greeting for the sun?

Here no blue and orange lamps burn
But sheep nudge aside the wool-faced sky.

Like the risen God of Easter
Our dreams like slippery births

twist as in the fecund earth, unchangeable.
Keeping both eyes safe

the wise one stumbles down
another crevice

another view of the moor
Figurations, solid and flighty as a dream

breathing through the mist, I lurch
Another interpretation

Anna Taylor

DRIVING UNTIL DARK

We two are in my car.
'Look at this' you say, 'Look there...',
polishing this hour.

Sails
of mist, of fine bleached linen, draw
threads of colour from the grass;
white waves
of small graves leap at their walls
in emptied fields. A horse
pearled with the mist – a cow –
slot into the window.
Now you sleep. The tyres
go 'fuss, fuss' along the road.

We dip and swerve until it's dark,
stop for a drink, swing over the hill
to a meadow of lights
twenty miles square.
Moorsides hide
behind the glare and lorries filled
with cigarettes, wool, scrap-iron, dirt,
blaze on the hilltop where they cart
Yorkshire into Lancashire.
The valley writhes, its sides
spitting and hissing. We slide,
like oysters down a throat, to Manchester.

Glyn Hughes

TO A PAIR OF BLUE EYES

Oh you whose eyes are sapphire swords of light
That flash to kill, or glance to wound a soul.
Lend me your blade and make of me your knight,
Take me into your arms and make me whole.
For as things are, I merely sit and wait,
I watch your eyes and know they do not see
The one who lives to make his soul your state,
He who would die to make his arms your fee.
A word, a look, a sigh would fill my cup,
Would wake and heal and make my life complete.
My life stands still until you raise me up.
My soul lies in the dust about your feet.
Take up that dust with love. Make me a man.
For nothing else can do what your eyes can.

FACES

Some only see your morning face my dear,
Bright from your sleep and eager for your way.
Some see your noontide face and they see clear
The toil that you have wrought so far this day.
Others your afternoon know best and see
All of your power displayed and strength on show.
You show your early evening face to me,
Then all your day has been I read and know.
But there are other faces that you keep
And show to none for long in case you give
Into their head a view or just a peep
Of all you are and love and how you live.
To me alone you grant a true love's right
To see and touch your secret face of night.

Howard Frost

MYVATN, ICELAND

For Valgerdur and Nils

What though their paths were never meant
to cross, as they to every sight
took the two parties they were sent,
the Germans claiming all by right,
the British more ambivalent?
No time for love to strike a light
and yet a few brief hours were spent
at Myvat Lake one starry night,
his bicycle beside her tent.

Let glacial waters roar their might
and Thor bestride the firmament.
Let laval outpours vent their spite,
the earth with fiery chasms rent.
Let warriors wake, renew their fight
in ancient feuds that came and went,
while elves waylay and trolls affright
For love brooks no impediment:
the bicycle will guard her tent.

Simon Currie

VERTEBRAE

Not of its own choosing,
the wind's edge, lusting in
to shift stones,
make woods and valleys howl.
See how today the tide is tipped.
A steep grey tongue
stretching for the dunes
to lap the marram grass
with here-ness.
Across oceans, boulders reach out,
their many coloured knuckles
rising naked, proud,
while wild rivers
thunder down between them.
Birds know their apex
just as an eel's sinew
drives it through meadows
to the furthest pond.

My love, our quiet bones are all these.

Pat Borthwick

Mowing, Ian M. Emberson.

About the Author – K. E. Smith

K E Smith was born in Leeds and went to school there and, later, in Bradford. At Belle Vue Boys' School he became aware that J B Priestley had been a student of the school half a century before and this heightened his own growing love of literature. Going on to study English at New College, Oxford, he was further inspired by his tutor John Bayley.

After a spell in Wales he returned to Yorkshire to teach at the University of Bradford. He joined the Pennine Poets in the 1970s and produced four books of his own poetry in the following decades, aiming to write in a manner at once modern yet accessible. He also became a widely-published literary critic, producing books on Cowper and Blake.

A strong commitment to Yorkshire's writers and language has always been important to him. In the 1990s he was editor of the long-established Yorkshire poetry magazine *Pennine Platform*, which has had close ties with the Pennine Poets group. Currently he is chairman of the J B Priestley Society for whom he has written several guides to Priestley's work. Most recently, he has focused on writing fiction set in the north of England.

He has recently been appointed the first Director of the English degree programme at the University of Bradford.

About the Editor – Pauline Kirk

Pauline Kirk is herself an author, poet and critic. Two novels – *Waters of Time* and *The Keepers* – and eight collections of her own poetry have been published, including *Walking to Snailbeach: Selected and New Poems*, which received excellent reviews. She is Senior Partner in the Fighting Cock Press, and has also edited local history and community publications. Her poems, short stories and articles have appeared in a wide range of journals and anthologies.

Born in Birmingham, Pauline moved to York in 2002, via Australia, Essex, Berkshire and Leeds. As a performance poet, she has appeared at venues throughout the country, and broadcast on Radio Leeds. In 1996 she received a 'New Beginnings' award from Yorkshire Arts to give up her 'day job' as a Senior Officer with Leeds Social Services. Herself a member of Pennine Poets, she now works as an editor and writer, and leads creative writing groups.

'Arum Maculatum', from *Imaginary Gates*, Mabel Ferrett,
2001, Wendy Cantell

Also published and available from
Fighting Cock Press
45, Middlethorpe Drive,
York YO24 1NA

The Imaginator,	Wendy Bardsley	£4.00
Remember Wyatt,	Nicholas Bielby	£5.00
Chernobyl's Cloud	Brian Blackwell	£2.50
Dunegrass,	Clare Chapman	£2.00
Doodles in the Margins of My Life,	Ian M. Emberson	£3.00
Natural Light, second edition,	Ian M. Emberson	£3.00
After Passchendaele,	Mabel Ferrett	£6.50
Imaginary Gates,	Mabel Ferrett	£4.00
Brian Merrikin Hill: Poet and Mentor,	Pauline Kirk	£2.00
Return to Dreamtime,	Pauline Kirk	£3.00
Brakken City,	Linda Marshall	£3.50
The Acts of St. Lynas,	Frank Pagden	£3.50
Kingfisher Days,	Mary Sheepshanks	£5.00
Thinning Grapes, 2nd edition,	Mary Sheepshanks	£6.50
Patterns in the Dark, 2nd edition,	Mary Sheepshanks	£5.50
On Wilsden Hill,	K.E.Smith	£1.50

Anthologies

Ho! Rumpelstiltskin,
ed. Pauline Kirk and Mabel Ferrett
£5.99

Pennine Poets: Anthology 1966-1986,
ed. Pennine Poets
£2.00

Pennine 25: Anthology 1966-91,
ed. Pennine Poets
£3.00

A Taste of the Pennine Poets,
ed. Pennine Poets
£2.00

Pennine Tracks,
ed. Clare Chapman
£3.95

Webbed Skylights of Tall Oaks,
ed. Clare Chapman
£4.95

In the same series as *Mind and Body*, and also supported by Arts Council England, Yorkshire, a Companion volume is available:

FIGHTING COCKS
Forty Years of Pennine Poets

SPIRIT AND EMOTION
BY
Mabel Ferrett
Edited by Pauline Kirk

A fascinating account of recent literary history. The Pennine Poets were and are a loosely affiliated group of genuine poets, individuals who have learned to be more themselves by learning from and supporting each other. The account is interleaved with poems by members of the group.

ISBN 0-906744-28-8
Price £12.50

For further information: www.penninepoets.co.uk

Other publications by K.E. Smith

Outcrop, Hewenden Editions, 1976.
(ed.) *Hopkins:Poetry and Prose*, Wheaton, 1976.
The Dialect Muse, Ruined Cottage Publications, 1979.
Slight Damage, Fighting Cock Press, 1980.
West Yorkshire Dialect Poets, Dialect Books, 1982
On Wilsden Hill, Fighting Cock Press, 1984.
Dialect Poets of the Dales, Dialect Books, 1987.
An Analysis of William Blake's Early Writings and Designs to 1790,
Edwin Mellen Press, 1999.
William Cowper: A Reappraisal, The Cowper and Newton
Museum, 2001.
Ancestral Memories, Feather Books, 2002
J.B. Priestley: A Spiritual Odyssey, J.B. Priestley Society, 2002.
(ed.) *Bright Day: A 60th Anniversary Celebration*, J.B. Priestley
Society, 2006.

By Pauline Kirk

Scorpion Days, Rivelin Press, 1982, Medal Poets (Australia), 1986.
(ed.)*Bramley: the Village that Disappeared*, Bramley History
Society, 1983 (and other local history booklets).
Red Marl and Brick, Littlewood Press, 1985.
Waters of Time, Century Hutchinson, 1988; Ulverscroft, 1991.
Rights of Way, Unibird Press, 1990.
(ed. with Brian Lewis) *Streets Ahead*, Yorkshire Arts Circus, 1994.
(ed.) *A Survivor Myself: Experiences of Child Abuse*, Yorkshire Arts
Circus, 1994.
Travelling Solo, KT Publications, 1995.
The Keepers, Virago (Little, Brown), 1996 and 1997.
Return to Dreamtime, Fighting Cock Press, 1996.
(ed.) *The Fairy Band*, by Walter Hill, KT Publications, 1997.
No Cure in Tears, Aireings Publications, 1997.
Brian Merrikin Hill: Poet and Mentor, Fighting Cock Press, 1999.
Owlstone, Thalia Press, 2002.
Walking to Snailbeach: Selected and New Poems, Redbeck Press,
2004.
(ed.)*Fighting Cocks Forty Years of Pennine Poets: Spirit and Emotion*,
Mabel Ferrett, Fighting Cock Press, 2006.
Faith Tea and Other Poems, The Parish Church of St. Edward the
Confessor, York, 2006.